AF271193

'Dispenses with the vast amount of marketing jargon and clearly lays out the foundations for marketing success.'

Matthew Housden, marketing consultant,
author, academic and trainer

'One of the most comprehensive marketing books that every student and practitioner should use to learn about the latest theories, tools and techniques to take their marketing potential to new heights.'

Ritchie Mehta, Founder and CEO, School of Marketing

'A straightforward, easy to understand marketing roadmap on how to thrive in our fast-changing times.'

Hap Klopp, Founder and former CEO of The North Face

'Comprehensive yet concise and insightful, *The Essentials of Contemporary Marketing* is highly engaging and easy to read. Key concepts balanced with practical applications provide a valuable resource to students or those seeking to better understand marketing.'

John Bredican, Teaching Fellow in Marketing,
King's College London

THE ESSENTIALS OF
CONTEMPORARY
MARKETING

MO WILLAN

BLOOMSBURY BUSINESS
LONDON • OXFORD • NEW YORK • NEW DELHI • SYDNEY

BLOOMSBURY BUSINESS
Bloomsbury Publishing Plc
50 Bedford Square, London, WC1B 3DP, UK
29 Earlsfort Terrace, Dublin 2, Ireland

BLOOMSBURY, BLOOMSBURY BUSINESS and the Diana logo are trademarks
of Bloomsbury Publishing Plc

First published in Great Britain 2021

Copyright © Mo Willan, 2021

Mo Willan has asserted his right under the Copyright, Designs and Patents Act,
1988, to be identified as Author of this work

All rights reserved. No part of this publication may be reproduced or transmitted
in any form or by any means, electronic or mechanical, including photocopying,
recording, or any information storage or retrieval system, without prior
permission in writing from the publishers

Bloomsbury Publishing Plc does not have any control over, or responsibility for,
any third-party websites referred to or in this book. All internet addresses given
in this book were correct at the time of going to press. The author and publisher
regret any inconvenience caused if addresses have changed or sites have ceased
to exist, but can accept no responsibility for any such changes

A catalogue record for this book is available from the British Library

Library of Congress Cataloging in Publication data has been applied for

ISBN: 978-1-4729-8857-7; eBook: 978-1-4729-6372-7

2 4 6 8 10 9 7 5 3 1

Typeset by Deanta Global Publishing Services, Chennai, India
Printed and bound in Great Britain by CPI Group (UK) Ltd, Croydon CR0 4YY

To find out more about our authors and books visit www.bloomsbury.com
and sign up for our newsletters

This book is dedicated to the memories of my father and mother with much love, respect, gratitude and admiration.

Contents

Overview

Like most disciplines, the practice of marketing is evolving on an almost daily basis, driven by advances in technological innovations as well as by changes in consumer behaviours. The local, international and global marketing environments in which companies operate are characterized by such continuous change, which implies that marketers need to also adapt, innovate and pivot their marketing activities in order to stay relevant, survive and succeed in such a challenging business landscape.

The outbreak of COVID-19 in 2020 decimated markets all over the world. The devastating effects of the epidemic have hit countries across the globe exceptionally hard, and almost every sector or industry is affected in one way or another. In the US, for example, at present still the world's leading economy, consumer spending declined by 12.6 per cent in the month of April 2020 alone, and many millions of people have been made jobless. Sectors such as retail, travel, hotels and restaurants have been decimated, with many downsizing operations or going out of business completely. At the other end of the scale, sectors such as online food retailing and home deliveries, and communication connectivity providers such as Zoom and Microsoft Teams, are witnessing surging consumer demand for their services.

At the time of writing in early 2021, consumer attitudes seem to be characterized by focusing on buying only essential products, a general unwillingness to interact and socialize, as well as maintaining tight controls over their spending habits. This implies that marketers are going to find it more difficult to convince consumers to make purchases, even when that pent-up demand is finally released. Simultaneously, many companies have resorted to reducing their marketing budgets in the face of such uncertainties and because of falling revenue. Therefore, the task for marketers in these challenging times – the effects of which are likely to be felt for at least the next few years – should be to market more effectively, strategically and compassionately by engaging in the following marketing activities:

- Brands will need to build relationships and trust by demonstrating to customers an authentically 'caring' attitude and by creating unique and special offers with high value.
- Continue with repetitive sincere, genuine and altruistic messaging. The objective is to capitalize on this opportunity to build unbreakable bonds with customers by showing that the brand cares more about them and their families than the company's profits.

Many leading brands moved swiftly to take proactive steps to stay engaged and connected to their audiences. For example, in March/April 2020, Nike asked consumers to 'play inside, play for the world'. It backed this messaging with a campaign that waived fees for premium programming on the Nike Training Club App. This implied that Nike was still inspiring people to be active during the global lockdowns, which is true to the brand, but doing it in a way that resonated with the sense of community that was required during the initial phases of the COVID-19 crisis.

The marketing challenge facing brands is in striking the right balance, which requires more than just snappy slogans. Consumers need to be reassured that their money is going towards companies that are doing – and being seen to do – the right thing. This implies that customers want to know whether the company's food products are sustainably sourced, for example, or how the company acted to protect its employees throughout the pandemic.

During most crises, marketing teams are often the first to be sacrificed, but the COVID-19 crisis – for now – seems to be different. By August 2020, Internet usage was up to almost 70 per cent on 2019 levels and while most customers might not be buying, they are at least engaging. The pandemic has no doubt changed the way people use and consume online content and services. Tolerance for screen time has never been greater and this is unlikely to change anytime soon. This would suggest that marketers need to revisit their approaches to organic traffic, where the focus should be on providing relevant content and building trust in other ways – especially considering that the pandemic has made it more difficult for consumers to visit physical stores. Updating the company's homepage on a regular basis, as well as responding to customers' concerns quickly and proactively, creating content that addresses such concerns, can go a long way towards fostering and reinforcing a sense of trust.

Marketing strategies, both during and after the pandemic, will need to refocus on using content to create powerful online connections. By humanizing the brand and speaking directly to consumer's interests, questions and concerns, companies can nurture an ongoing conversation, even among those who may find themselves in challenging financial situations. Support is not always tied to revenue; if the quarantine has taught us anything, it is that online conversations can be just as meaningful as face-to-face interactions, and marketers need to take note of this.

The aim of this book is to provide readers with a simple, easy to understand and succinct introduction to the theories, concepts and practices of marketing. The author's motivation for writing the book is based on feedback received from the many students who commented that most of the currently available marketing textbooks were too bulky, not sufficiently reader-friendly and overloaded with too much detail. Hence, the goal of this new book is to provide readers – especially those who are new to the discipline of marketing, or who find themselves needing to know more about the marketing function as part of a new role – with concise and topical explanations of the essential marketing concepts, theories and practices.

The book is divided into three broad sections, namely:

The first chapters of the book focus on providing an understanding of what the discipline of marketing entails, as well as an appreciation of the marketing environment, which affects marketing decisions and practices. This part delves into how the discipline of marketing has evolved, as well as looking at some of the issues that are shaping modern-day marketing. It then discusses the marketing environment in which companies operate: marketing decisions are rarely taken in a vacuum but rather are shaped by changes in the firm's environment and its interactions with multiple stakeholders. Successful marketing very much relies on having a sound understanding of the context in which the organization operates. As such, marketers need to be prepared and equipped to address changes that are constantly happening in the business world by scanning the marketing environment and making appropriate responses and changes to their marketing plans.

The second part of the book covers consumer behaviours, marketing research and segmentation, targeting and positioning, which helps in a clearer understanding of how consumers make their purchasing decisions and how such information can be gathered. Considering that gaining an understanding and appreciation of how consumers think and behave serves as the bedrock of marketing decisions and practices, this area is critical for marketing success. In turn, understanding consumers leads to marketing research, which enables marketers to gather the best information upon which any marketing decisions are based. The concept and practice of segmentation, targeting and positioning, which enables firms to serve distinct subsets of the broader market, is especially crucial in modern business practice, given that traditional forms of mass marketing are on the wane.

The final chapters cover marketing in practice. These include the marketing mix, marketing planning and international marketing. The marketing mix is the 'heartbeat' of marketing practice, as it enables marketers to develop and apply the *right* product at the *right* price in the *right* place with the *right* promotions, by hiring the *right* people to deliver the *right* process with the *right* physical evidence, decisions and practices when serving the needs of consumers. Initially, there were only four Ps commonly discussed – namely: Product, Price, Place and Promotion – but these have now evolved into the seven Ps so as to include People, Process and Physical evidence. Achieving marketing success implies that all these aspects of the marketing mix should be well coordinated and blended to produce an integrated action plan that ensures the attainment of brand and organizational success. Failure to get it right with the execution of any of the individual elements of the marketing mix will lead to the potential failure of some or all of the other elements.

This is followed by a look at marketing planning, which specifies how marketers define and outline their objectives and thus develop relative and appropriate strategies to achieve those set marketing objectives. Planning is extremely critical because it sets out at a very early stage how the firm will go about attaining its objectives – it may be a cliché, but failing to plan means planning to fail.

The final part of the third section delves into global or international marketing. The most successful firms today are also the most global. Brands such as Apple generate more than 60 per cent of revenues outside of its home market, the USA. Coupled with advances in technologies, vanishing trade barriers and homogeneous consumer characteristics, firms are now finding it easier than ever to enter foreign markets where they can achieve higher levels of brand awareness, increase consumer demand, and to generate more sales and profits.

CHAPTER ONE

Introduction to Marketing

To study any subject, first start by gaining a fundamental understanding of it. Marketing is one of the most misunderstood of subjects. For most people who have not studied it before, their understanding of marketing revolves around words such as 'advertising', 'selling', 'promotion' and so on. In as much as selling and advertising constitute part of marketing, however, the study of marketing transcends selling and advertising. The two most widely used definitions of marketing are the ones put forward by The Chartered Institute of Marketing and The American Marketing Association.

The Chartered Institute of Marketing (CIM), the largest professional marketing organization, defines marketing as:

> The management process concerned with identifying, anticipating and satisfying customer requirements efficiently and profitably (CIM, 2015)

This definition entails four key components, namely:

1) **Identifying customers' wants**
   The management of the organization should consistently seek to understand what customers want and then develop the right products and services to meet and satisfy those wants. This involves engaging in continuous market research in order first to find out and determine as much as possible what exactly the wants of customers are and then to put in place the right strategies and tactics to address and satisfy such customer wants. Amazon has been very successful in

this regard by developing products and services that are affordable, easy accessible online and delivered to customers quickly at their doorsteps.

2) **Anticipating customers' wants**

The needs and wants of customers are never the same all the time. In fact, customer wants change all the time. Therefore, the ability of the firm's management to project the future wants of customers is paramount to marketing success. Failing to foresee, capture and address consumers' ever-changing wants will make the firm's products redundant. Blockbuster Video is a classic example of failing to project that consumers were migrating towards digital platforms for watching films as opposed to borrowing video tapes!

This can also involve creating needs for customers. Indeed, many firms today tend to develop products and then convince consumers to buy even though their customers had never thought before that they needed such products.

3) **Satisfying customers' wants**

This aspect of the marketing definition builds on and is the culmination of the first two components. Customer satisfaction implies that the firms produce the right products, at the right price, in the right place with the right promotional messages. It also entails that the service involved in delivering the product is fast, easy to understand and convenient for customers, and that the environment in which the product is delivered or served is comfortable, conducive and welcoming. Customer satisfaction is the bedrock of effective marketing and can yield two possible outcomes:

- Satisfied customers will come back, repurchase the product and recommend it to at least three other people. This ultimately translates into customer loyalty and higher rates of profitability for the firm. Existing customers' recommendations are considered the best advertising for the firm because it is free and more trustworthy than the firm's own communications.

- Dissatisfied customers will not repeat purchase from the firm and will relate their dissatisfaction to at least seven other people. The implication of this is that the firm will lose much needed sales income as well as sustain damage to the brand.

It is important to distinguish between customers and consumers. Whereas consumers are the actual users of the products, customers can be people who actually buy the products. For example, a mother buying diapers or toys for her baby is the customer but the baby is the consumer of the product. In many cases, a customer can also be the consumer as in the case of women buying make up, but consumers are deemed the most influential on purchase decisions.

The American Marketing Association defines marketing as:

'. . . the activity, set of institutions, and processes for creating, communicating, delivering, and exchanging offerings that have value for customers, clients, partners, and society.' (AMA, 2013)

The AMA definition explains that marketing should serve a much broader purpose than simply serving the actual needs of individual customers but rather should also incorporate meeting the needs of the different stakeholders, including partners and the wider society in which the firm operates. This is in line with the societal marketing concept, which implies that firms should endeavour to produce products that meet and satisfy the needs and wants of both customers and the society.

This definition also places heavy emphasis on creating and delivering value to stakeholders. Value in this context means benefits for all the pertinent stakeholders, such as employees, shareholders, suppliers, customers, government and society. Each of these different stakeholders should benefit from the activities of the firm in different ways – jobs for employees, dividends for shareholders, products for customers, tax revenue for governments and investment in the societies in which the firm operates.

Evolution in the Practice of Marketing

Over the years, marketing has evolved from a transactional exchange focusing on single sales and interactions with customers to becoming more relationship-focused. Relationship marketing places heavy emphasis on building and maintaining long-term mutually beneficial relationships with customers. There are a number of trends that will continue to impact on the practice of marketing as it further evolves and moves into the future. These trends include the following:

- **The Internet and connectivity**

  In recent years, the Internet has transformed the way organizations provide their products and services and how consumers interact with brands. Advances in technological developments, globalization, consumer confidence in the security of financial payment systems, and changing consumer lifestyles with an increasing emphasis on convenience have all contributed towards the growth of online interactions between organizations and their consumers. Consumers of Generation Z are digital natives, who are most comfortable interacting with organizations using digital technologies and expect firms to provide such platforms, enabling them to interact at all times and wherever they are.

- **Ethical Consumption**

  Growing consumer concerns for environmental issues and sustainability will continue to influence consumer behaviours, and firms must factor this into their decision-making and strategies. The related issue of Corporate Social Responsibility (CSR) implies that firms must be good, active and responsible citizens, showing genuine concern for the well-being of both the societies in which they operate and the wider world. This issue of environmental friendliness and consideration is especially important if firms are to succeed in attracting the millennial generation, who attach a heavy emphasis to issues of environmental protection.

- **Growing Importance of Capturing Consumer Data**

  Marketing success very much depends on understanding consumers. This calls for firms to invest, develop and harness consumer data with the objective of better identifying and addressing consumer needs. The use of marketing metrics is important and should be based on first capturing critical consumer data and then implementing mechanisms designed to measure marketing efficiency and effectiveness.

Functions of Marketing

Marketing is one of the most important functions in any organization. This is because it serves the critical purpose of ascertaining customers' wants and producing the right products and services that the firm offers to consumers, which in turn generates sales and ultimately profits. The functions of marketing include the following:

- Determining the most efficient and effective marketing strategies that will contribute towards the achievement of the firm's objectives. This includes determining the types of customers that the firm should target and serve and facilitating exchange relationships with such customers.
- Creating strategies for the positioning of the firm and its products. This implies crafting effective communications that will be effective in creating positive brand perceptions in the minds of its stakeholders
- Scanning the business environment continuously to identify possible opportunities and likely threats and how to exploit such opportunities and mitigate the threats.
- Conducting market research to ascertain customer wants and communicating these internally so that the firm is in a better position to address these ever-changing customer needs and wants. Market research recommends the right products and services for the firm to offer its customers to make it relevant and competitive. This will include a consideration for such critical issues as product, price, place, promotion, people, process and physical evidence (together, these are often referred to as the 7Ps).
- Determining the firm's basis for competitive differentiation and advantage. This implies that the marketers should contribute towards making the firm and its products unique relative to its competitors, and

is arguably the most challenging function of marketing, especially in highly competitive markets.

- Measuring and evaluating the effectiveness or otherwise of the firm's marketing activities. This involves measuring whether the firm's set marketing objectives have been attained or not. If not, why not? What can be done moving into the future to correct any anomalies? Such objectives may include increasing market share and profitability.

Criticisms of Marketing

Despite the important function played by marketing in the success of organizations, it is a practice that has also been criticized. These criticisms include the following:

- Marketing encourages people to buy things that they do not need. This is often achieved by means of intense advertising and promotions.
- Marketing creates waste through the overproduction of goods that are often thrown away when not sold. This leads to environmental waste, which has gained a lot of traction and importance in modern-day business practice.
- Marketing encroaches on customer's privacy with the sending of unsolicited messages, the sharing of customer data and in recent times the actual losing of customer data to hackers.
- Marketers embellish product claims in order to make customers buy the firm's products. Arguably, this is one of the most significant negative aspects of the marketing function, especially in the cosmetics and vitamins products industries
- Marketing discriminates in customer selection. Some firms are very specific in terms of the types of customers they wish to attract and serve. Though this is legal and also smart from a business point of view, it is considered by others as unethical, creating and dividing people into 'classes'.

CHAPTER TWO

Marketing Orientations

Marketing as a discipline is quite broad and different firms adopt different approaches in terms of how they practice it. Market orientation in its simplest form refers to the approaches or philosophies that underpin how firms will go about meeting and satisfying the needs of their customers.

There are typically five different orientations, namely:

1) Product orientation
2) Production orientation
3) Sales orientation
4) Marketing orientation and
5) Societal orientation

Product orientation

The firm's approach is based on producing products that are superior to the competition. Firms that adopt this approach invest heavily in research and development and are consequently able to develop products with unique features and better qualities that will ultimately attract customers to the product. Dyson, which manufactures vacuum cleaners, hairdryers and hand dryers, is a classic example of a modern-day firm that practises product orientation.

Production orientation

With this type of orientation, the firm focuses on achieving production efficiencies and lower operational costs that are ultimately transferred to customers in the form of lower prices for its products. Typically, such firms tend to produce large volumes of the same product or limited product range and the emphasis is on leveraging economies of scale to produce such products at the lowest possible costs. There is often little consideration for the requirements of customers. This is based on the premise that the low prices offered due to lower production costs are the prime considerations that will attract customers. Henry Ford, who founded the Ford Motor Company, made this approach popular with the Model T.

Sales orientation

This type of orientation entails that the firm puts heavy emphasis on selling what the firm produces, regardless of customer requirements. This is often necessitated because the supply exceeds demand for the firm's products. As a result, the firm focuses and embarks on aggressive advertisements, sales promotions and personal selling in order to sell its products. Such firms believe that with aggressive advertisements, sales promotions and personal selling, customers can be convinced to buy its products. Highly trained salespeople are sent out by the firm to meet customers in the streets or in their homes to push its products to customers, irrespective of customer demand or requirements.

Some credit card firms, broadband service providers and double-glazing firms tend to adopt this approach.

Marketing orientation

This approach is based on the firm focusing and putting its customers at the heart of all its marketing activities. Market research is critical, first in determining customer requirements and then in producing products that meet and satisfy such requirements. In practical terms, marketing orientation can be achieved by the following:

- An understanding of customer needs throughout the organization
- Strong, in-house marketing training programs
- The hiring of strong marketing talent
- Continuous review and monitoring of marketing performance
- A Chief Executive who echoes the voice of the customer
- Strategies reflecting the market
- Marketing being considered more important than other functions
- A responsiveness to marketing opportunities
- Good marketing information systems
- The use of marketing research
- A link between marketing and new product development
- Marketing being considered as everyone's business
- Coordinated and integrated marketing decisions

Firms that adopt this approach can benefit from a strong understanding of customer requirements and ultimately better customer relationships. Such relationships can foster customer loyalty, competitive advantage and profitability. The Swedish retailer H&M is a classic example of a firm that puts a heavy emphasis on researching customer requirements first and then producing products that meet those requirements.

Societal orientation

This approach is an extension of marketing orientation. It puts the emphasis on not only addressing customer requirements but also on ensuring that marketing solutions enhance the well-being of the society in which the firm operates. In other words, this approach focuses on the firm producing products that specifically meets its customers' requirements and which at the same time do not have a negative effect on society. Aspects of societal well-being include a consideration for such issues as pollution and recycling. The Body Shop, which sells ethically sourced and cruelty-free products, prides itself on being a societal oriented company.

Questions

Choose a company of your choice and then explain and justify the most appropriate market orientation it should adopt in the marketing of its products.

'In 2021 and beyond, firms need to adopt societal orientation if they are to succeed in the marketing of their products.' Critically analyse this statement.

CHAPTER THREE

The Marketing Environment

Analysing and understanding the marketing environment is an important prerequisite for identifying customer needs and wants and a successful marketing practice. Organizations exist and operate in complex and ever-changing environments, and these changes can either present opportunities for the organization to exploit or pose a threat to the success or survival of the organization. Such environments can be local, national or even global.

There are many players and actors in the environment, and these include suppliers, intermediaries, customers, competitors, governments and other stakeholders. Thus, the marketing environment can be defined as consisting of many forces and actors that are predominantly outside marketing but which can affect the organization's ability to develop and maintain mutually beneficial relationships with its targeted customers.

'Environmental scanning' is a process undertaken to identify, monitor, analyse and respond to the forces in the firm's environment which can affect its performances. It involves:

- Monitoring the trends, key events and pertinent issues that can affect the firm
- Identifying the factors that can significantly impact the firm's operations
- Evaluating or assessing the impact of these factors on the company
- Forecasting likely scenarios to determine both opportunities and threats

Environmental scanning therefore implies that firms should consistently gather information on the issues and events happening around them to respond appropriately. Such information gathering exercises are critical to the firm's ongoing planning processes and also serve as a basis for determining likely opportunities and threats facing the firm.

Environment information can be obtained from the following sources:

- The firm's own records, such as sales records
- Newspaper and journal articles
- Marketing research agency reports from such recognized organizations as Euromonitor, Nielsen, Mintel and Keynote
- The websites of major news organizations such as Bloomberg or CNN
- Reports prepared by consultancy firms such as BCG, Bain and McKinsey
- Reports from trade unions
- Reports prepared by trade organizations
- Reports from international bodies such as the World Trade Organization reports
- Government reports such as the census report
- Company websites
- Social media platforms and discussion forums

The business and marketing environments can be divided into three – the internal environment, the micro-environment and the macro-environment.

The Internal Environment

The internal environment, as the name implies, is composed of those elements or actors that exist within the organization and which can affect, and be affected by, the activities of the firm. These actors will typically include employees and managers, as well as other resources within the organization. It is worth pointing out that the firms will have considerable leverage and control over the actors within its internal environment. Aspects of the internal environment include a consideration for the following:

- Products, services and brand reputation
- The capabilities of employees and managers
- Financial resources
- The state of production facilities
- Research and development capabilities

To analyse and better understand the internal environment, marketing managers can use and apply a number of analytical techniques, including:

- SWOT Analysis
- McKinsey's 7S Framework
- The Boston Consulting Group (BCG) Matrix

SWOT Analysis

This is an overall evaluation of a company's *Strengths, Weaknesses, Opportunities* and *Threats*. Strengths and Weaknesses are internal and can be controlled by the organization while Opportunities and Threats are external forces that firms cannot control. The objective of SWOT analysis is to identify and convert threats into opportunities and weaknesses into strengths. When applying the SWOT analysis for the purpose of internal analysis, the emphasis should be on the strengths and weaknesses which are internal and can be controlled by the firm. Strengths refer to an organization's capabilities or aspects of its business that it does better than its competitors. For example:

- Coca-Cola has a strong brand name
- Marks and Spencer is noted for its high-quality products
- Virgin is known for its high levels of customer service
- Apple is known for its product innovation

Weaknesses refer to aspects of an organization's activities in which it may not excel. For example:

- Lidl is sometimes criticized for its lack of in-store customer service
- McDonald's is an easy target for the 'junk food' label.

Opportunities are aspects in the business environment that the organization can either capitalize upon or take advantage of. Opportunities can include the firm entering new markets and/or developing new products. For example:

- Tesco using its huge customer database to diversify into non-grocery products such as insurance, credit cards and loans.
- Walmart using its brand strength and financial muscle to enter into new markets/countries

Threats are aspects in the business environment which pose a challenge or can hamper the organization from achieving its objectives. For example:

- Competitors
- Changing consumer needs
- Government legislations
- Natural disasters such as earthquakes or floods

Positive	Negative
Strengths	**Weaknesses**
Technological skills	Absence of important skills
Leading Brands	Weak brands
Distribution channels	Poor access to distribution
Customer Loyalty /	Low customer retention
Relationships	Unreliable product / service
Product Quality	Sub-scale Management
Scale Management	
Opportunities	**Threats**
Changing customer tastes	Changing customer tastes
Liberalization of geographic	Closing of geographic
markets	markets
Technological advances	Technological advances
Changes in government	Changes in government
policies	politics
Lower personal taxes	Tax increases
Change in population age-	Change in population age-
structure	structure
New distribution channels	New distribution channels

Internal Factors (rows: Strengths / Weaknesses)
External Factors (rows: Opportunities / Threats)

Figure 1: SWOT Analysis

TOWS Analysis

This helps marketers identify strategic alternatives that address the following additional questions:

- Strengths and Opportunities (SO) – How can the firm use its strengths to take advantage of the opportunities?
- Strengths and Threats (ST) – How can the firm take advantage of its strengths to avoid real and potential threats?
- Weaknesses and Opportunities (WO) – How can the firm use its opportunities to overcome the weaknesses you are experiencing?
- Weaknesses and Threats (WT) – How can the firm minimize its weaknesses and avoid threats?

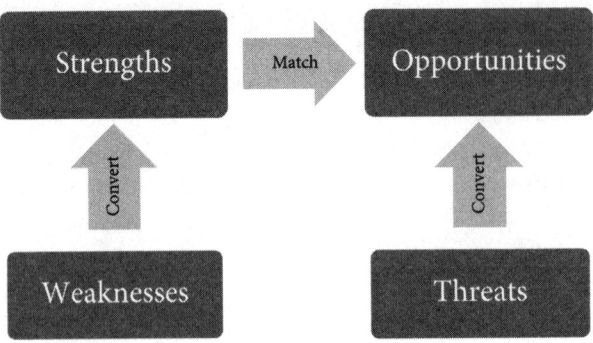

Figure 2: TOWS Analysis

The McKinsey 7S Model

The McKinsey 7S Model is a framework for organizational effectiveness. It postulates that there are seven internal factors that need to be aligned and reinforced in order for an organization to be successful. The model depicts the interdependency of the elements and indicates how a change in one affects all the others. The McKinsey 7S framework provides a useful approach to organizational design, specifically for:

- Facilitating organizational change
- Aligning the organization to new strategy
- Aiding the merger or acquisition of organizations
- Improving the performance of a company
- Modelling the likely effects of future changes within a company.

It poses key considerations or questions to organizations and managers in charge of decision-making and implementing change. These include the following:

- Is there senior support to review the organization's design?
- Are the seven elements of the framework aligned with each other?
- What is the best organizational design to support the objectives?
- What needs to change to achieve the best organizational design?
- Do you have the necessary resources to bring about the changes identified?

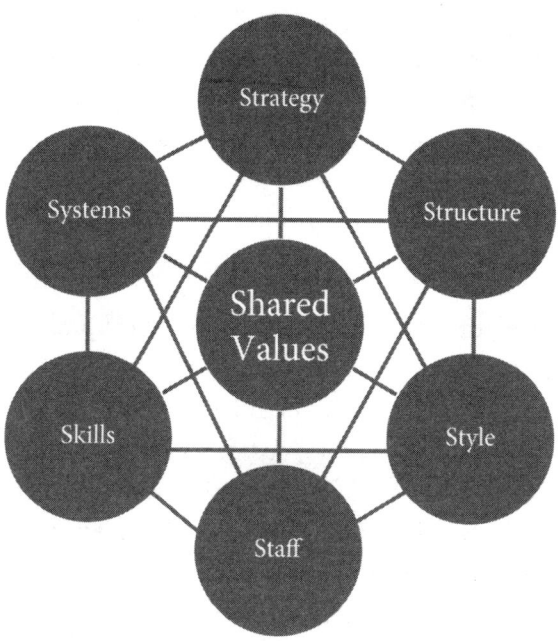

Figure 3: McKinsey's 7S Framework

The seven interdependent elements of the framework are:

1) Strategy – the plan devised to maintain and build competitive advantage over the competition.
2) Structure – the way the organization is structured and who reports to whom. It denotes the levels of responsibility and authority within the firm – who is who and who does what within the company.
3) Systems – the daily activities and procedures that staff members engage in to get the job done. Systems are the area of the firm that determines how business is done, and it should be the focus for managers during organizational change.
4) Style – the style of leadership adopted. Leadership styles can be democratic, participative or autocratic in nature.
5) Staff – the employees and their general capabilities.
6) Skills – the actual skills and competencies of the employees working for the company.

7) Shared Values – called 'superordinate goals' when the model was first developed, these are the core values of the company which are evidenced in the corporate culture and the general work ethic. They are the norms and standards that guide employee behaviour and company actions and thus are the foundation of every organization.

Micro-Environmental Analysis

The micro-environment consists of players, actors and forces that exist within the firm's industry and which can to some extent affect the firm's abilities to serve its customers. The micro-environment includes such players as suppliers, distributors, customers and competitors. To help in analysing and understanding the micro-environment, marketing managers can apply the Porter's Five Forces Framework. The five forces are environmental forces that affect a company's ability to compete in a given market. The purpose of five-force analysis is to diagnose the principal competitive pressures in a market and assess how strong and important each one is.

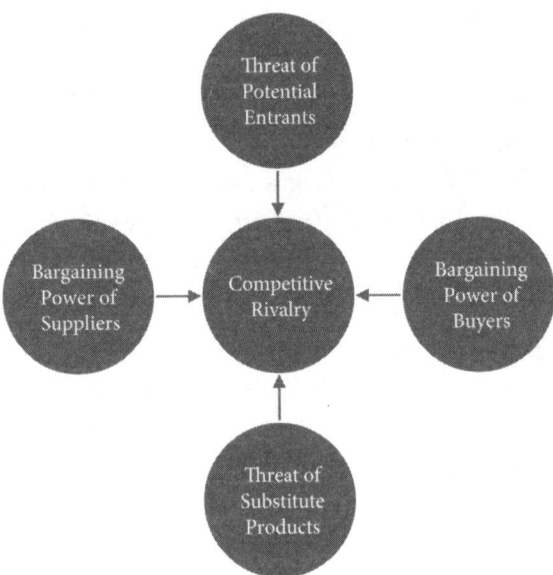

Figure 4: Porter's Five Forces Framework

The Bargaining Power of Buyers

Buyer power will also tend to reduce profitability and depends on such factors as:

- The importance of the product as a proportion of the total purchases of the buyer
- The cost of switching to alternative suppliers
- Buyer concentration and size
- The emphasis given by the buyer to product differentiation and branding
- Knowledge of the market and information available to buyers
- Existence of substitutes

The Bargaining Power of Suppliers

Where the relative power of suppliers is considerable and their behaviour aggressive, the rate of profits in the industry will be squeezed. However, an ability to establish control over suppliers will strengthen the hand of the business in the industry. The main factors determining relative power of suppliers include the following:

- The number and relative size of supplier
- The ability to switch to rival suppliers and the cost involved
- The importance of being unimportant – the lower the cost of the supplies as a proportion of the total cost, the higher the bargaining power
- The threat of forward integration by suppliers.

The Availability of/Threats of Substitute Products

Substitutes are either direct or indirect products that can be alternated in place of other products. For example, a direct substitute for McDonald's is Burger King and its indirect substitutes can be KFC, Nando's and Pizza Hut. Factors affecting the threat of substitutes include:

- The relative price of the substitute product
- Switching costs
- The buyer's willingness to search out substitutes

The Threat of New Entrants

Any profitable industry is susceptible to this threat, particularly where a recent improvement in returns has occurred. Thus, long-run profitability and market share will be affected if significant market entry occurs. However, there are factors that may delay or even prevent the threat of new entrants:

- Economies of scale
- Government policies
- Brand loyalty
- Capital requirements
- Distribution channel access
- Expected retaliation

The Rivalry among Existing/Competing Firms

Rivalry in the industry can range from non-existent (monopolies) or courteous understandings (collusive oligopoly) to a cut-throat price war. The degree of rivalry can be determined by such factors as:

- The cost of leaving the industry
- The volatility of supply and demand
- Misinterpreting competitor's intentions – unintended price wars
- What is at stake – if survival is threatened/big investment involved

Competitor Analysis

Competition is a modern fact and reality in business today. There are few industries where competition does not exist. As a result, marketers must continuously study, monitor and respond to competitive pressures. Competitor analysis is a critical part of a firm's activities. It is an assessment of the strengths and weaknesses of current and potential competitors, which may encompass firms not only in their own sectors but also in other sectors. Directly or indirectly, competitor analysis is a driver of a firm's strategy and impacts on how firms act or react in their sectors. Competitor analysis, together with an understanding of major environmental trends, is a key input in strategy formulation and should be developed properly.

In utilizing competitor analysis as part of strategy formulation, firms are able to adapt or build their own strategies and compete effectively, improve performance and gain market share. In a large number of instances, firms are able to tap new markets or build new niches.

The key objectives of competitor analysis are to develop a greater understanding of what competitors have in place in terms of resources and capabilities, what they plan to do in their businesses, and how the competitors may react to various situations in reaction to what the firm does. Porter has defined a competitor analysis framework that focuses on four key aspects:

Competitors' Objectives

In competitor analysis, there are two key factors to note when building knowledge of a competitor's objectives. The first factor is to know the actual objectives of a competitor. This could range from building market share in a specific market or overall business, entering a new market or even just maintaining profitability. The second factor is to know if the competitor is actually achieving their stated (or sometimes unstated but implied) objectives. Looking at these two factors will provide marketers with an idea on a competitor's potential actions to changes in the sector.

As part of a comprehensive competitor analysis piece, firms should identify their key competitors and be able to define the objectives of each competitor and their likelihood of achieving their objectives.

Some of the questions to ask for the competitor's strategic objectives are:

- What are the short-term and long-term objectives?
- Where is the competitor investing?

Competitors' Assumptions

Another key aspect in competitor analysis is an understanding of competitors' assumptions about the overall market (trends in the market, products and consumers). For example, competitors could define their actions based on their assumptions about the growth of the market. For a proper competitor analysis work, the assumptions made by competitors should be indicated, but the validity of those assumptions should be challenged.

Some questions to address include:

- What is the competitor's perspective on the market and development?
- Who are the key consumers or clients believed by the competitor to be most profitable?

Competitors' Strategy

A third aspect in competitor analysis is the understanding of a competitor's strategy. In most cases, this strategy will be clearly defined and stated, particularly in the case of public firms. In other cases, it may not be openly stated as regards, but these can be understood by utilizing a number of sources available to firms, from analysing a competitor's behaviour in certain situations to discussions with industry experts.

Questions to address include the following:

- What are the strategy and plans of competitors in their key markets?
- Which markets and products will the competitor focus on?

Competitors' Resources and Capabilities

Finally, competitor analysis should also include an understanding of a competitor's resources and capabilities because these will give a firm an idea of how a competitor can achieve its strategy and objectives, and give a firm a timeline for when it expects competitors to pursue certain activities. For this aspect, a large part of information can be gleaned from press articles and news.

Several questions that can be raised in this respect are:

- What is the level of resources available to the competitor for their investments?
- What are the areas of strength for the competitor?

Macro-Environmental Analysis

The macro-environment consists of forces that are outside a marketer's control. These forces are constantly changing and can open up opportunities to firms or present threats to firms. Firms must therefore continuously monitor, adapt and respond to these dynamic forces.

The PESTLE analysis is mainly used to analyse the wider macro-environment in which the business operates. The organization will normally have no control over PESTLE factors and at best should try to accommodate and devise strategies around them. The PESTLE acronym describes the following factors or forces:

P = Political
E = Economic
S = Sociocultural
T – Technological
L = Legal
E = Environmental or Ecological

Political Factors

Players in the political environment includes governments, government departments, industry bodies, pressure groups as well as political parties. These groups affect an organization and its operations in different ways. The philosophy of the government in power sets the business climate in which firms operate. Political factors that can affect businesses include a consideration of the following:

- The political stability prevailing in the country – firms do not thrive in politically unstable countries and will often choose to withdraw. Libya is an example from recent years.
- The political orientation of the government in power – democratic or autocratic?
- The incidence of strikes, which can cripple firms. Where strikes are prevalent, as in countries like France, this can affect the willingness of firms to invest in the country.
- The attitude of government officials – a number of Western governments seem to be pursuing an increasingly hostile strategy towards China. This can discourage firms in such countries from investing in China.
- Government policies such as immigration and taxation policies.

Economic Factors

The buying and selling of goods and services that prevail in any given country can no doubt impact upon the firm's operations. These factors are determinants of an economy's performance that directly impacts a company and have resonating long-term effects. For example, a rise in the inflation rate of any economy would affect the way companies price their products and services. Adding to that, it would affect the purchasing power of a consumer and change demand/supply models for that economy. Economic factors include the following:

- Interest rates affect firms because many firms borrow from financial institutions to invest and grow the business. Consumers are also affected by rates of interest charged on credit cards and personal loans. Higher levels of interest might discourage firms from borrowing and consumers from spending on their credit cards.

- Employment levels may indicate that people have jobs and money to spend on the firm's products and services. This can also affect the cost of hiring for the firm, as high unemployment will make labour costs cheaper.
- Inflation rates can affect the operating costs of firms as prices in general tend to go up, which will compel the firm to increase its own prices and ultimately affect its competitiveness.
- Disposable incomes indicate the monies that people have to spend.
- The economic cycle – is the country in recession or going through an economic boom? This can affect the firm's pricing decision for example
- Taxation can affect prices for products and services and ultimately consumers' ability and willingness to spend.

Sociocultural Factors

These factors refer to both the social and cultural norms that prevail in countries in which the firm operates and are especially important for marketers when targeting certain customers. In addition, it also says something about the local workforce and its willingness to work under certain conditions. Sociocultural factors include the following:

- Population demographics such as size, density, age and gender profiles
- Lifestyles such as leisure-time activities and patterns of social interactions
- Levels of education, both in terms of people's skills levels and ability to understand the firm's communication message
- Religions practiced in the country – for example in strict and conservative Muslim countries such as Saudi Arabia, the public sale of alcohol is forbidden
- Aesthetics, such as the meaning of colours, numbers and artefacts
- Language in terms of the interpretation of words in different cultural contexts
- Attitudes and values that shape people's perceptions and behaviours

Technological Factors

These factors pertain to innovations in technology that may affect the operations of the industry and the market favorably or unfavorably. These factors may, for example, influence decisions to enter or not enter certain industries, to launch or not launch certain products or to outsource production activities abroad. By knowing what is going on technology-wise, the firm may be able to prevent itself from spending a lot of money on developing a technology that would become obsolete very soon due to disruptive technological changes elsewhere. Technological factors include the following:

- Government spending on research to promote the development of products and services that are technology related
- Government and industry focus on technology such as the licensing of 5G networks
- Communication infrastructure and technologies such as the availability of broadband, television and radio station for advertising purposes
- Transportation infrastructure – availability of road networks, rail networks, airports and sea ports, which can affect the movement of people and product
- Technological skills to support and power existing and new innovations

Legal Factors

Although these factors may have some overlap with the political factors, they include more specific laws such as discrimination laws, antitrust laws, employment laws, consumer protection laws, copyright and patent laws, and health and safety laws. It is clear that companies need to know what is and what is not legal in order to trade successfully and ethically. If an organization trades globally this becomes especially tricky since each country has its own set of rules and regulations. In addition, you want to be aware of any potential changes in legislation and the impact it may have on your business in the future. Legal considerations should include the following:

- Monopolies legislation, which can deter new competitors from entering specific industries. In many African countries, the supply of electricity is strictly regulated and managed by governments only and not open for private sector participation.
- Foreign trade regulations such as free trade agreements. For example, The European Union allows for the free movement of people, goods and investments, which encourages trade between its 26 member states.
- Employment law such as payment of minimum wages
- Health and safety laws especially in such industries as airlines and food service providers

Environmental / Ecological Factors

Environmental factors have come to the forefront only relatively recently. They have become important due to the increasing scarcity of raw materials, pollution targets and carbon footprint targets set by governments. Furthermore, growing awareness of the potential impacts of climate change is affecting how companies operate and the products they offer. This has led to many companies getting more and more involved in practices such as corporate social responsibility (CSR) and sustainability. These should include a consideration of the following factors:

- Environmental protection laws. For example many countries are now banning the use of plastic bags
- Consumer activism, from campaigning groups such as Friends of the Earth
- Green issues, such as the production of organic products
- Social responsibility can impact the firm's business practices, such as paying fair prices to suppliers for any raw materials, payment of fair wages to workers and making positive contributions to the betterment of the societies in which firms operate.

Questions

As a marketing manager, you have been asked to evaluate the sales potential for your chosen company's products in a newly identified overseas market. Why should you conduct a SWOT and PESTLE analyses? Prepare a report explaining the roles of these analyses and why you have chosen to conduct them.

The macro-environment consists of forces that are outside a marketer's control. These forces are constantly changing and can open up opportunities to firms or present threats to firms. Firms must therefore continuously monitor, adapt and respond to these dynamic forces.

For each of the following macro-environmental issues, explain how the firm should respond and adapt its marketing activities:

- Increase in the rate of taxation levied on the firm's products.
- A new competitor entering the market that the firm you have chosen currently operates in.
- A new political party coming to power in a given country that your chosen firm operates in.
- The chosen country is experiencing high levels of unemployment.

CHAPTER FOUR

Consumer Behaviour

As explained in the first chapter, marketing is all about identifying and satisfying the needs of consumers, so understanding customers is crucial to marketing success. The Customer is King, so it is of critical importance that organizations devote significant time and resources to understanding their customers. It is essential to gain a solid understanding of what customers buy, why they buy, how they buy and when they buy. It is also crucial to understand the differences between consumers (users of the firm's products) and customers (buyers of the firm's products) because it can be the case that buyers are not always the users – it can be mothers who buy clothing for their children, for example.

Consumer behaviour is the study of the decision-making process that consumers go through in their purchasing decisions. Companies need to ensure that they tailor their marketing activities and efforts to match the behaviours of consumers.

The study of consumer behaviour involves both business-to-consumer (B2C) and business to business consumer markets (B2B). Business to consumer implies that the organization sells to individual consumers and business-to-business implies that the organization sells to other organizations.

The Consumer Decision-Making Process (B2C)

Consumers typically go through a number of distinct stages in their buying decisions, and this is known as the consumer decision-making process. The diagram below illustrates the different stages involved:

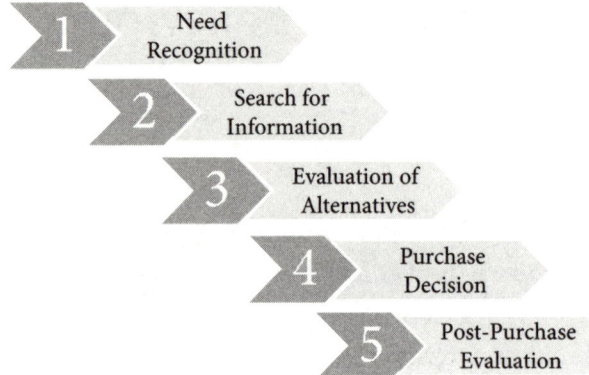

Figure 5: Consumer Decision-Making Process

Need or Problem Recognition

The first stage of the decision-making process implies that the potential customer has a need or problem that is to be satisfied. This need can be brought about by internal factors such as hunger for food, or by external factors such as company promotions for its products. The implication for marketers is that understanding such customer need will enable the firm to better serve these needs.

Information Search

Once the need is established, consumers will begin to search for the necessary information in order to satisfy the need. Sources of information can include past experiences, recommendations from friends and family, company commercials and promotions and, in more recent times, online sources, endorsements from celebrities and experts and reviews from past consumers.

Evaluation of Alternatives

After gathering information from available sources, the consumer will compare the different products that can potentially satisfy their particular needs. This includes a consideration for both direct and indirect competing products. The product comparison factors may be based on different criteria, vary from consumer to consumer, and can include price and payment terms, product features, quality perceptions, image consciousness, ethical values and delivery terms.

Purchase Decision

At this stage, the consumer has already compared the different products that can potentially satisfy their need and is ready to commit and buy the product. This purchase can involve visiting the store or distribution outlet or buying online. Again, the purchase decision can be influenced by the same factors as for the previous stage, the Evaluation of Alternatives.

Post-purchase Decision

This is the stage where the consumer compares the extent to which the purchased product has actually satisfied their need. This stage is of critical importance because it determines the likelihood of future purchases by the consumer and their recommendation to others. Satisfied consumers will typically recommend the product to three other people, and dissatisfied ones will tell at least seven others. Word of mouth recommendation is considered the best advertisement for a company, as it is often considered more trustworthy by consumers, and for the company it costs nothing!

Cognitive dissonance tends to set in at this stage: the buyer has doubts and conflicting thoughts about whether they have made the right choice. This can be reduced on the part of the consumer by focusing more attention to information that supports their choice of product or by ignoring information that undermines their choice.

The extent to which consumers adopt and apply the decision-making process depends on the level of involvement in the purchase. The level of involvement means the extent to which the purchase is important to the buyer. For example, for everyday products such as chewing gum, consumers will not typically go through all the five steps explained, and this is considered low involvement. However, when it comes to buying a car or choosing a university, consumers engage in high involvement and will typically go through all five stages of the decision-making making carefully and invest a lot of time and effort in the process.

The level of involvement is influenced by four factors, namely:

- **Self-image** – the extent to which the consumer believes the product will affect how they view themselves, such as the car they drive or the clothes they wear.
- **Perceived risk** – every purchase involves a risk, meaning that the product might not meet the consumer's expectations. There are different types of risks involved in purchasing decisions and actions. Financial risk relates to how expensive the product is. Physical risk relates to the inherent dangers in using the product. Functional risk to the possibility the product might not work. Social risk to the concerns of how others might respond. Psychological risk to how making a wrong purchase can affect the psyche of the consumer (making them look stupid).
- **Social factors** – this relates to how the purchase can affect the consumer's social standing and how other members of the society may judge them.
- **Hedonism** – the extent to which the consumer believes that the purchase will deliver high levels of pleasure, such as flying first class.

Types of Buyer Behaviours

Consumers' purchase decisions can also be affected by the differences they perceived in competing products. This leads to four different types of buyer behaviours:

	High involvement	Low involvement
Significant differences between brands	Complex Buying Behaviour	Variety-seeking Buying Behaviour
Few differences between brands	Dissonance-reducing Buying Behaviour	Habitual Buying Behaviour

Figure 6: Types of Buying Decision Behaviours

1) **Complex buying behaviour** – consumers in this category will typically invest a lot of time and effort in learning about the product they are buying while going through the different stages of the decision-making process. They also display high levels of involvement with the product and will go as far as comparing and learning about the differences in the brands they intend to buy. An example of such complex buyer behaviour is when shopping for a car.

2) **Dissonance-reducing buying behaviour** – such consumers think that there are minor differences between competing brands under purchase consideration and hence do not typically invest a great deal of time and effort in their shopping. These consumers will exhibit high levels of involvement but also think that all competing brands are more or less the same. Buying low-cost airline tickets is an example.

3) **Variety-seeking buying behaviour** – such consumers are predominantly driven by the need to try something different in their purchasing decisions. They make a conscious decision to try different products in the same category and tend to display low levels of involvement but appreciate the differences between products. The purchase of fast food can be an example.

4) **Habitual buying behaviour** – this is also known as the routine buying of frequently bought products and implies that such

consumers spend very little time thinking about such purchases. There is low involvement, and consumers believe there are very little differences between competing products. The purchase of bread is an example.

Factors Influencing Consumer Buying Behaviours

To be better able to address and serve consumers' ever-changing needs, marketers must devote time and resources to identifying and, more importantly, understanding the factors that influence consumers' buying behaviours. There are a number of factors that influence consumers' buying behaviours and these include a consideration for the following:

1) **Personal factors** – the individual attributes or characteristics of consumers, such as age, gender, income, occupation and lifestyle. For example, consumers' income levels will greatly affect the types of products they can afford to buy.

2) **Cultural factors** – these are learned from family and society, and have a huge effect on consumer behaviours. Such aspects include religion, values, laws, social roles, education, language and social organization. For example, neither Jews nor Muslims eat pork based on their religious beliefs.

3) **Social factors** – such issues and considerations as family, social class and reference groups. In many societies, family members consult one another when making purchases for products. The use of celebrities is also another example of how reference groups influence consumers' purchasing decisions.

4) **Psychological factors** – human psychology does play an important role in determining consumer's preferences. Psychological factors include perceptions, learning, motivations, attitudes and beliefs. Learning relates to the fact that consumer's previous experiences with a product can affect their behaviours towards such products.

Perception affects behaviours based on the process of how consumers select, organize and interpret sensory stimulation such as sounds, vision, smell and touch into a coherent and meaningful picture of the world. Marketers use music in advertising to make consumers think or to evoke emotions relative to their products (classic conditioning). Motivation explains the reasons why consumers buy certain products; the higher the level of motivation, the greater the need to buy the product that satisfies that motivation. Finally, attitudes and beliefs are derived from knowledge, opinion or faith – for example, a consumer who believes in healthy eating will strive to avoid junk food.

Organizational Buying Behaviour (B2B)

There are distinct differences between B2C and B2B markets and these differences include the following:

- The volumes of purchase are much larger in B2B markets than B2C markets
- The frequency of purchase is often less in B2B markets due to the larger quantities purchased
- There are many people involved in the purchasing decisions in B2B markets. These people involved includes users, buyers, approvers and gatekeepers (such as financial controllers who may specify purchases from specific sources)
- Demand is usually inelastic in B2B markets
- Products can be customized in B2B markets
- The decision-making process takes a much longer time in B2B markets due to the many people involved in the process
- Negotiation is common in terms of prices and delivery terms in B2B markets
- Experts are involved in the B2B decision-making process

The Organizational Buying Process

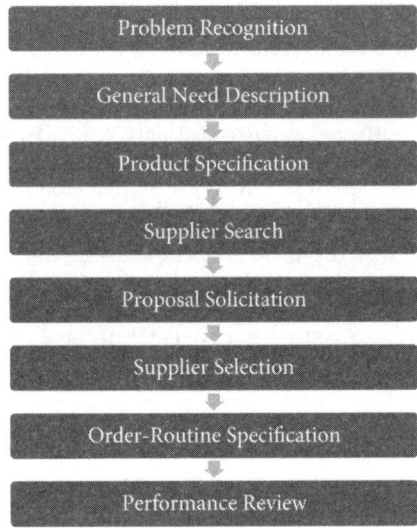

Figure 7: Organizational Buying Process

As compared to the individual consumer decision-making process, organizational buying processes take longer and are more complex.

Problem recognition
People or groups of people within the organization identify a problem that needs to be solved by buying a particular product or service.

Product Specification
Once the product need is identified, the organization will determine the characteristics of the product to be bought to solve the problem. The characteristics or attributes of the product can include a consideration for quality, performance level or compatibility with existing systems. The opinions of experts within the organization are also sought in determining such product attributes.

Supplier Search
Following on from the product specification, the organization will begin searching for potential suppliers for the product. Suppliers can

be sought from existing organizations that have already done business with the organization or from organizations recommended by employees, trade directories, online searches or promotional materials.

Proposal Solicitation

This involves inviting potential vendors or suppliers to submit proposals outlining how their products and services meet the organization's specified products sought. The proposals will typically explain such issues as price, delivery terms, aftersales services, reordering processes, etc.

Supplier Selection

After the submitted proposals from the potential suppliers are reviewed, the organization will make a decision about the most suitable supplier to work with in terms of producing and supplying the product.

Order Specification

This stage involves the organization making a commitment to the purchase by placing orders for the product from the chosen supplying organization.

Performance Review

This stage involves the buying organization assessing the performance of the product in terms of the extent to which it meets the identified problem. This is important in terms of determining whether the organization will reorder from the same supplying organization in the future.

Factors Influencing Organizational Buying Behaviour

There are a number of internal and external factors that influence organizational buying behaviours. These factors are outlined below:

- **Individual Factors**

  B2B decisions are influenced by the characteristics of the individuals involved in the selection process. A person's job position tenure, and level in the organization may all influence a purchasing decision. Additionally, a decision-maker's relationships with peers and managers may lead them to exert more – or less – influence over the final selection. An individual's professional motives, personal style, and credibility as a colleague, manager, or leader may all play a role.

- **Organizational Structure**

  Purchasing decisions, especially big-ticket expenditures, may be influenced by the organization's strategies, priorities and performance. Generally the decision-makers and the providers competing for the business must present a compelling explanation for how the new purchase will help the organization become more effective at achieving its mission and goals. If a company goes through a quarter with poor sales performance, for example, the management team might slow down or halt purchasing decisions until performance improves. An organization's existing systems, products or technology might also influence the buying process when new purchases need to be compatible with whatever is already in place.

- **Current Financial Situation**

  The financial position of the firm can no doubt influence what it can afford to buy. High levels of profitability mean that the firm is in a position to spend more, but in lean periods the firm may cut back on spending.

- **Organizational Goals and Objectives**

  The goals and objectives explain what the firm aims to achieve. This may include investments in procuring and developing new products and services.

- **Government and Regulatory Changes**

  Government and the regulatory environment can also influence purchasing decisions. Governmental organizations often have very strict, highly regulated purchasing processes to prevent corruption, and companies must comply with these regulations in order to win government contracts and business. Similarly, lawmakers or governmental agencies might create new laws and regulations that require organizations to alter how they do business – or face penalties.

In these situations, organizations tend to be highly motivated to do whatever it takes, including purchasing new products or altering how they operate, in order to comply.

- **Competition**

  Changes in the competitive environment can also influence a firm's buying decisions. It could be the case that existing competitors or new entrants in the market are offering a product or service that necessitates the firm to introduce new products or services. This will compel the firm to buy similar and use similar products and services.

The study of consumer behaviour implies that marketers can influence consumers through each of these stages, depending on the marketing activities undertaken.

Marketing A Luxury Brand in Japan – Louis Vuitton

Overview of the Japanese Luxury Market

In recent times, Japan has become the capital of luxury brands. It remains the world's second-largest luxury market, with consumers spending £19 billion on luxury goods in Japan in 2018, according to Bain. Deloitte predicts that Japan's luxury market will continue to grow steadily to 2022, with the increasing number of professional women also spurring sales. Revenue in the Luxury Goods market is projected to reach US$30,464m in 2021. The market is expected to grow annually by 4.3 per cent for the period 2021–2025. The market's largest segment will be the segment Prestige Cosmetics & Fragrances, with a market volume of US$14,210m in 2021 (*Vogue Business*, 2018).

Japan represents the biggest market for luxury brands such as Bulgari, Burberry, Baccarat, Gucci and Louis Vuitton representing up to half of their sales globally. Quality had always been a key factor for successful brands in Japan, especially for smaller brands or niche brands that did not enjoy the same sort of success as larger brands such as Louis Vuitton. However, new, foreign brands are trying to penetrate the market and gain market share from the bigger and more well-known luxury brands in Japan by offering high-quality products at competitive prices. As a result, the effectiveness of the business models of brands such as H&M, Zara and Uniqlo completely transformed the market within a short period. Affordability is a concept that is radically changing the mindset of Japanese customers, who were always eager to resemble top fashion models from famous catwalk shows.

Consumer Behaviour in Japan

Japan is known for a group-orientated culture in which there is a real pressure to own luxury status-driven brands. Successful brands such as Prada, Hermes and Louis Vuitton had made the Japanese luxury market into a mass market.

The Japanese way of consumption is markedly different from the western one. The proportion of the urban population in Japan that owns a famous, expensive luxury brand item is immense, reflecting a tendency not as deeply ingrained in other developed cities such as New York, London or even Paris, which is often seen as the high-end capital of luxury fashion. The Japanese way of consuming cosmetics and luxury brands is more like a compulsory form of social expression.

According to Davide Sesia, President of Prada Japan, Japanese women, to a much greater extent than Europeans, have a 'psychological need to own something considered to be beautiful'. The cultural and social characteristics among Japanese society may go some way to explaining its attachment to luxury products. The existence of a large middle class and a high population density certainly affect buying habits, and people are used to spending more time outside of their homes than people in many other parts of the world. As such, Japanese society can be described as an 'impersonal' society, in which personal aesthetics and appearances are considered very important and people often feel pressured to dress in a manner that corresponds to their social status or position in society.

Yet, times are changing and Japanese consumers are becoming less inclined to tolerate the high prices that had previously created desirability. Although young Japanese women would still be eager to save money for the 'it' brands, they are becoming more aware of the value of money; lower-priced accessories and small leather items such as wallets are becoming increasing popular. Japanese consumer mindsets are also changing as the market evolves towards more sophistication, and luxury brands are no longer purchased as symbols of membership in the new urban class. The norms of mature brand behaviour and changing consumer habits seen in the western world are now starting to be reflected in the Japanese luxury market. Davide Sesia reflects that 'The increasing attitude of Japanese women in their 20s and 30s to understanding themselves much better than in the past is a key phenomenon.' As a result, in the luxury market, the ready-to-wear segment has clearly been very affected by the new trends in Japanese women's buying choices.

Conclusion

The global COVID-19 pandemic hit economies all over the world, and Japan is no different. There are signs that young Japanese women do not have the same vision, outlook or perceptions as previous generations. They are no longer eager to buy expensive products and many luxury brands are already suffering the consequences. As such, luxury brands such as Louis Vuitton will have to reinvent themselves to be able to reposition themselves as contemporary brands that can adapt to and exploit the changing consumer behaviours seen in the Japanese market.

Question

Examine the concept of consumer buying behaviour, and analyse the issues affecting Japanese consumers' buying behaviours towards the Louis Vuitton brand.

CHAPTER FIVE

Market Research

Market research refers to the systematic process of collecting, analysing and presenting research data in relation to a specific problem facing an organization. As discussed in an earlier chapter, market research can be conducted to address any of the 7Ps – namely Product, Price, Place, Promotion, Process, People and Physical Evidence. Market research plays a very important role because:

1) It eliminates many risks in management decision-making because decisions made will be based on facts and not assumptions.
2) It enables management to make better informed decisions.

The Market Research Process

The market research process explains the various steps involved in conducting a marketing research project. This process is collectively known as the DODCAR Framework:

D = Define the research problem
O = Objective setting
D = Design the research plan
C = Collect the research data
A = Analyse the research data
R = Report or present the research findings

D = Define the Research Problem

Market research is needed when decision makers must make a decision but lack the information to help them do so. Market research is needed to determine if problems exist, to generate, refine and evaluate marketing actions and to evaluate marketing performance. It is also needed to determine if there are opportunities in the market. This is the most important step in the market research process because all the subsequent steps are very much influenced by the nature of the research problem or the need for the research.

O = Objective Setting

Research objectives are determined by the research problem which, when achieved, provides the necessary information to solve the research problem. A good way of setting research objectives is to ask, 'What information is needed in order to solve the Problem?'

Research objectives identify what specific pieces of information are necessary to solve the research problem at hand.

D = Design the research plan

Designing the research involves the various issues that need to be considered for the successful implementation of the research. These are:

- The research methods chosen
- The cost of the research
- The time period involved in conducting the research
- Who will do the research – an in-house team or external research agencies?
- The research sample and the size of the sample
- The methods for collecting the research data
- The types and sources of information
- The methods to be used for analysing and presenting the data

C = Collect the Research Data

Research data can be collected from two main sources, namely primary and secondary data sources. Primary data is information collected specifically for the study under consideration. Secondary data is data collected for another purpose not specifically related to the proposed research and which is already in existence. Primary data can be obtained by means of questionnaires and interviews. (Turn to the end of this chapter, page 46, for an in-depth analysis of the various methods of obtaining primary data).

A = Analyse the Research Data

Once data is collected, data analysis is applied to give the raw data meaning. Data analysis involves entering data into computer files, inspecting the data for errors and running tabulations and various statistical tests (for quantitative data), and finally using other means of analysis and summary (qualitative data) to find out what the data reveals. In most social research, the data analysis involves three major steps, done in roughly this order:

1) **Data Preparation**, which involves checking or logging the data in; checking the data for accuracy; entering the data into the computer; transforming the data; and developing and documenting a database structure that integrates the various measures.

2) **Descriptive Statistics**, which are used to describe the basic features of the data in a study. They provide simple summaries about the sample and the measures. Together with simple graphics analysis, they form the basis of virtually every quantitative analysis of data. With descriptive statistics you are simply describing what is – i.e. what the data shows.

3) **Inferential Statistics** investigate questions, models and hypotheses. In many cases, the conclusions from inferential statistics extend beyond the immediate data alone. For instance, inferential statistics are used to try to infer from the sample data what the population thinks. Or to

make judgments of the probability that an observed difference between groups is a dependable one or one that might have happened by chance in this study. Thus, inferential statistics are used to make inferences from the data to come up with conditions that are more general.

R = Report Research Findings

The final stage of the marketing research process is to prepare and present the final research report. Preparing the marketing research report involves describing the process used, building meaningful tables and using presentation graphics for clarity. The research report can be presented in any of the following forms:

- Tables
- Graphs
- Charts
- Oral presentations
- Combination of any or all of the above

Methods Of Obtaining Primary Data

Questionnaires

A questionnaire is a document containing questions and other types of items designed to solicit information appropriate for analysis. Questionnaire questions could be of two types, namely:

1) **Open-Ended Questions** – for which the respondent is asked to provide their own answers.
2) **Closed-Ended Questions** – for which the respondent is asked to select an answer from among a list provided by the researcher.

Rules in Questionnaire Design

- Questions should be relevant
- Short items are best
- Avoid negative items

- Avoid biased items and terms
- Make items clear
- Avoid double-barrelled questions
- Respondents must be competent to answer
- Respondents must be willing to answer

Interviews

A data-collection encounter in which one person (the interviewer) asks questions of another (the respondent). Interviewers offer the following benefits:

- Soliciting higher response rates (80–85 per cent) than mail surveys.
- Minimizing 'don't know' and 'no answer'.
- Serving as a guard against confusion.
- Observing respondents while completing the questionnaire.

Types of Interviews

A researcher has to conduct interviews with a group of participants at a juncture in the research where information can be obtained only by meeting and personally connecting with a section of their target audience. Interviews offer researchers the opportunity to prompt their participants and obtain inputs in the desired detail. There are three fundamental types of interviews in research:

Structured Interviews

Structured interviews are defined as research tools that are extremely rigid in their operations, allowing very little or no scope for prompting the participants to obtain and analyse results. It is thus also known as a standardized interview and is significantly quantitative in its approach. Questions in this interview are pre-decided according to the required detail of information.

Structured interviews are extensively used in survey research with the intention of maintaining uniformity throughout all the interview sessions.

They can be closed-ended as well as open-ended – according to the target population. Closed-ended questions can be included to understand user preferences from a collection of answer options whereas open-ended can be included to gain details about a particular section in the interview.

Advantages of structured interviews

- Structured interviews focus on the accuracy of different responses, which also enables the collection of extremely in-depth data. Different respondents have different type of answers to the same structure of questions – the answers obtained can be collectively analysed.
- They can be used to get in touch with a large sample of the target population.
- The interview procedure is made easy due to the standardization offered by structured interviews.
- Replication across multiple samples becomes easy due to the same structure of interview.
- As the amount of detail can be considered while designing the interview, better information can be obtained and the researcher can analyse the research problem in a comprehensive manner by asking the most accurate and effective research questions.
- Since the structure of the interview is fixed, it often generates reliable results and is quick to execute.
- The relationship between the researcher and the respondent is not formal, which allows the researcher to identify the margin of error where the respondent either refuses to be a part of the survey or is just not interested in providing the appropriate information.

Disadvantages of structured interviews

- Limited scope of assessment of obtained results.
- The accuracy of information overpowers the detail of information.
- Respondents are forced to select from the provided answer options.

- The researcher is expected to adhere to the list of decided questions irrespective of how interesting the conversation is turning out to be with the participants.
- A significant amount of time is required for a structured interview.

Semi-structured Interviews

Semi-structured interviews offer a considerable amount of leeway to the researcher to probe the respondents while maintaining a basic interview structure. Even if the conversation is guided, researchers enjoy an appreciable flexibility.

Keeping the structure in mind, the researcher can follow any idea or take creative advantage throughout the interview. Additional questions help garner further information. The best application of the semi-structured interview is when the researcher does not have time to conduct research and requires detailed information about the topic.

Advantages of semi-structured interviews

- Questions for semi-structured interviews are prepared before the scheduled interview, which provides the researcher with time to prepare and analyse the questions.
- Interviews are flexible while also maintaining the research guidelines.
- Researchers can express the interview questions in the format they prefer, unlike the structured interview.
- Reliable qualitative data can be collected via these interviews.
- Flexible structure of the interview.

Disadvantages of semi-structured interviews

- Participants may question the reliability of these interviews due to the flexibility offered.
- Comparing two different answers becomes difficult, as the guideline for conducting interviews is not entirely followed. No two questions will have the exact same structure and the result will be an inability to compare results.

Unstructured Interviews

Also called 'in-depth interviews', unstructured interviews are usually described as conversations held with a purpose in mind – to gather data. These interviews have the least number of questions as they lean more towards a normal conversation but with an underlying subject.

The main objective of most researchers using unstructured interviews is to build a bond with the respondents, offering a high chance that the respondents will be 100 per cent truthful with their answers. There are no guidelines for the researchers to follow, so they can approach the participants in any ethical manner to gain as much information as possible.

Since there are no guidelines for these interviews, a researcher must be mindful of their approach so that the respondents do not sway away from the main research motive. For a researcher to obtain the desired outcome, he/she must keep the following factors in mind:

- The intent of the interview.
- The participant's interest and skills.
- All the conversations should be conducted within permissible limits of research.
- The skills and knowledge of the researcher should match the purpose of the interview.
- Researchers should understand the dos and don'ts of unstructured interviews.

Advantages of Unstructured Interviews

- The informal nature of unstructured interviews makes it extremely easy for researchers to develop a friendly rapport with the participants. This enables them to gain insights in extreme detail without much conscious effort.
- Participants can clarify all their doubts about the questions and the researcher can take each opportunity to explain his/her intentions to achieve better answers.

- There are no specific questions for the researcher to ask and this usually increases the flexibility of the entire research process.

Disadvantages of Unstructured Interviews

- As there is no structure to the interview process, researchers take time to execute these interviews.
- The absence of a standardized set of questions and guidelines indicates that the reliability of unstructured interviews is questionable.
- In many cases, the ethics involved in these interviews are considered borderline.

Research Interview Methods

There are three methods to conduct research interviews, each of which is peculiar in its application and can be used according to the research study's specific requirements.

Personal Interviews

Personal interviews are one of the most used types of interviews, where the questions are asked personally directly to the respondent. For this, a researcher can have an assistant take note of the answers. A researcher can design his/her survey in such a way that they take notes of the comments or points of view that stands out from the interviewee.

Advantages of Personal Interviews

- Higher response rate.
- When the interviewees and respondents are face to face, the questions can be adapted if not readily understood.
- More complete answers can be obtained, along with unexpected insights.
- The researcher has an opportunity to detect and analyse the interviewee's body language in response to questions.

- Among the advantages of conducting these types of interviews is that the respondents will have more fresh information if the interview is conducted in the context and with the appropriate stimuli, so that researchers can have data from their experience at the scene of the events, immediately and first hand. The interviewer can use an online survey through a mobile device that will undoubtedly facilitate the entire process.

Disadvantages of Personal Interviews
- They are time-consuming and extremely expensive.
- They can generate distrust on the part of the interviewee, who may be self-conscious and not answer truthfully.
- Contacting the interviewees can be a real headache – either scheduling an appointment in workplaces or going from house to house and not finding anyone at home.

Telephonic Interviews
Telephonic interviews are widely used and easy to combine with online surveys to carry out research effectively.

Advantages of Telephonic Interviews
- To find the interviewees, it is enough to have their telephone numbers on hand.
- They are usually lower cost.
- The information is collected quickly.
- The personal contact can also clarify doubts or give more details for each question.

Disadvantages of Telephonic Interviews
- Often people do not answer phone calls because it is an unknown number for the respondent, or respondents may have changed their place of residence and cannot be located.
- Researchers also encounter respondents who simply do not want to answer, perhaps fearful of putting their own security at risk.

- Interviewers should be careful to address the respondents politely in order to secure their cooperation. Good communication is vital for generating better answers.

Email or Web Page Interviews

Online research is becoming increasingly important because consumers continue to migrate to a more virtual world and it is best for researchers to adapt to this change.

Research via email or web pages are most used today, and for this nothing is better than an online survey.

Advantages of Email Surveys
- Speed in obtaining data.
- The respondents respond in their own time, at the time they want and in the place they decide.
- Online surveys can be mixed with other research methods or previous interview models.
- Researchers can use a variety of questions and logics, then create graphs and reports immediately.

Undoubtedly, the objective of the research will set the pattern for what types of interviews are best for data collection. Based on the research design, a researcher can plan and test the questions to ensure that the questions are correct and that the survey flows smoothly.

To summarize, an effective interview will be one that provides researchers with the data that is the object of the study, and which is most relevant and applicable to the decision makers.

Sampling

Collecting research data includes using people as samples. Sampling is the process of selecting units (e.g., people, organizations) from a population of interest so that by studying the sample we may fairly generalize our results back to the population from which they were chosen.

There are two basic sampling techniques:

1) Probability sampling
2) Non-probability sampling

Probability Sampling

A probability sampling method is any method of sampling that utilizes some form of *random selection*. For a random selection method, you must set up some process or procedure to ensure that the different units in your population have equal probabilities of being chosen. The basis of probability-based random sampling is that every member of the population must have a known, non-zero chance of being selected. Probability sampling provides the means by which the margin of sampling error can be calculated and the level of confidence in survey estimates reported. Sampling errors result from collecting data from some rather than all members of the population and is highly dependent on the size of the sample.

Types of Probability Sampling Techniques

1) **Random cluster sampling** is a way to select participants randomly, spread out geographically. For example, to choose 100 participants from the entire population of the United States, a researcher will randomly select areas (i.e., cities or counties) and then randomly select from within those boundaries. Cluster sampling usually analyses a particular population in which the sample consists of more than a few elements – for example, city, family, university, etc. Researchers then select the clusters by dividing the population into various smaller sections.

2) **Stratified random** sampling is a probability sampling procedure in which the target population is first separated into mutually exclusive, homogeneous segments (strata), and then a simple random sample is selected from each segment (stratum).

3) **Cluster sampling** is a probability sampling procedure in which elements of the population are randomly selected in naturally occurring groupings (clusters). In the context of cluster sampling, a 'cluster' is an aggregate or intact grouping of population elements. Element sampling is the selection of population elements individually, one at a time. On the other hand, cluster sampling involves the selection of population elements not individually but in aggregates. The sampling units or clusters may be space based, such as in terms of naturally occurring geographical or physical units (e.g., states, counties, census tracts, blocks or buildings) or organizations (school districts, schools, grade levels or classes).

4) **Systematic sampling** is when the researcher chooses every 'nth' individual to be a part of the sample. For example, you can select every fifth person to be in the sample. Systematic sampling is an extended implementation of the probability technique in which each member of the group is selected at regular periods to form a sample. There is an equal opportunity for every member of a population to be selected using this sampling technique.

Process of Conducting Probability Sampling

The following steps outline the process of conducting probability sampling:

1) **Choose your population of interest carefully.** Think carefully and choose from the population those people whose opinions you believe should be collected, and then include them in the sample.

2) **Determine a suitable sample frame.** The sample frame should consist of a sample from your population of interest and no one from outside it, to ensure the collection of accurate data.

3) **Select the sample and start the survey.** It can sometimes be challenging to find the right sample and determine a suitable sample frame. Even if all factors are in your favour, there still might be unforeseen issues like cost, the quality of respondents

and their quickness to respond. Getting a sample to respond to a probability survey accurately may be difficult, but it is not impossible.

When to Use Probability Sampling

1) **When you want to reduce the sampling bias:** This sampling method is used to minimize bias. How researchers select their sample largely determines the quality of the findings. Probability sampling leads to higher quality findings because it provides an unbiased representation of the population.

2) **When the population is usually diverse:** Researchers use this method extensively because it helps them create samples that fully represent the population. Say we want to find out how many people prefer medical tourism over treatment in their own country: this sampling method will help pick samples from various socio-economic strata to represent the broader population.

3) **To create an accurate sample:** Probability sampling help researchers create accurate samples of their population. Researchers use proven statistical methods to draw a precise sample size to obtained well-defined data.

Non-Probability Sampling

Non-probability sampling implies that not all the potential respondents have an equal chance of being selected.

Types of Non-Probability Sampling Techniques

1) **Convenience Sampling** is a non-probability sampling technique where samples are selected from the population only because they are conveniently available to the researcher. Researchers choose these samples because they are easy to recruit, and the researcher does not try to select a sample that represents the entire population. Ideally, in research, it is good to test a sample that represents the

population, but sometimes the population is too large to examine and consider the entire population. Then researchers rely on convenience sampling, which is the most common non-probability sampling method because of its speed, cost-effectiveness and ease of availability of the sample.

2) **Purposive / Judgemental Sampling** is a method by which researchers select the samples based purely on the researcher's knowledge and credibility. In other words, researchers choose only those people they deem fit to participate in the research study. This is not a scientific method of sampling, and the downside is that the preconceived notions of a researcher can influence the results. Thus, this research technique involves a high amount of ambiguity.

3) **Snowball Sampling** helps researchers find a sample when they are difficult to locate. Researchers use this technique when the sample size is small and not easily available. It works like a referral program: once researchers find suitable subjects, they ask for assistance to seek similar subjects, to form a good sample size.

4) **Quota Sampling** divides the population into strata or groups. Suppose a researcher wants to study the career goals of male and female employees in an organization. There are 500 employees in the organization, also known as the population. The researcher will need only a sample, not the entire population. Further, the researcher is interested in particular strata within the population.

When to Use Non-Probability Sampling

- To identify if a particular trait or characteristic exists in a population.
- To conduct qualitative research, pilot studies or exploratory research.
- When time is limited or there are budget constraints.
- When the researcher needs to observe whether a particular issue needs in-depth analysis.
- When the researcher does not intend to generate results that will generalize the entire population.

Eco Refill Systems – The Future of Packaged Oil

The California-based company Eco Refill Systems (ERS) was inspired by the US state's concerns around recycling, waste management and environmental stewardship, as well as the founder's unyielding passion and desire for sustainability. Bernadette Sarouli had worked in a packaging firm in the San Francisco area until June 2015. Her office window used to face the back of a building, where she saw deliveries and garbage pick-ups all day long. It dawned on her how many oil containers, cartons and pallets came in and out of their food service provider's kitchen. Her curiosity consumed her to such an extent that, as early as 2012, she had already started doing her own research and development on new designs with the goal of eliminating waste. She discovered that those plastic oil containers were unrecyclable and often ended up in landfill due to their exposure to air contaminants. Worse still, all of these oil containers and packaging waste occupied huge volumes in landfill, let alone the water bottles that form islands in our oceans. 'I thought [a lot] about this huge problem but I remembered how David defeated Goliath. In my mind I believed I could do something about the problem.'

Armed with her patented stainless steel *fustis* – a highly-polished, stainless steel container – Bernadette quit her job after three years of research and development. Still in the San Francisco area, she and her husband Lane Landry placed beta designs for their company, Eco Refill Systems, LLC. Somewhere in the process, however, they discovered something more significant in the cooking oil distribution system in particular.

The problem was about not only the plastic oil jugs but also all the related packaging that inhibited these items from being recycled once they were exposed to air contaminants and residual oil. The food service industry would never spend more than they have to in order to sanitize these units and packaging; as a result, Bernadette's company moved to integrate delivery and distribution into its business so that food service providers who placed orders would only have to turn the spout of the stainless steel *fustis* and let the right amount of oil drip into the cooking pan. This was the inception of the closed oil distribution system, which meant total convenience to service food providers, and for the same cost, but without the hassle and waste involved when using traditional plastic oil jugs.

The company's goal is to eliminate all packaging wastes in the delivery of cooking oil to food service centres in the San Francisco area by providing a closed oil distribution system, which guarantees that delivery is done directly from bulk storage to kitchen users. This system radically eliminates any use for packaging. Eco Refill Systems delivers and replaces empty oil *fustis* as often as any food service provider may require it. Bernadette then went to Twitter San Francisco and presented her service to their cafeteria. She had not even finished her proposal when Twitter's director concluded, 'This is a no brainer. We're on board with this.'

Today, the company counts among its clients such big corporations as Twitter, LinkedIn and Salesforce, as these companies all operate big kitchens within their offices to provide food and to cater for their employees. The company also serves local restaurants, hospitals and schools in the San Francisco area, and its business model at present is mainly focused on business-to-business clients.

Currently the business is restricted to the San Francisco area, although it continues to grow steadily. Already, the company has been able to eliminate over 14,000 plastic gallon containers annually from being abandoned to landfill, not counting the associated plastic lids and labels, the contaminated carton packaging and any residual oil, which are eliminated altogether. The business has no competition at present but still has some way to go in engaging the food service industry to reconsider its green practices. However, Bernadette and Lane are passionate about their quest to use their closed oil distribution system to take down a Goliath in terms of systemic environmental degradation.

ERS's goals are to refill, re-use and restore. Of these is a striking statement that comes from the 'restore' part: 'Our vision captures the ideal of food waste returning to the farmers whose hands and backs nurture the earth. Our incredible *fustis* … solve many of the common concerns and dangers in food service kitchens, including cost, mobility, space, and freshness.' Made in Italy with seamless artisanship, its patented *fustis* are available in a variety of sizes to fit unique kitchen needs. The company provides weekly or bi-weekly refillable oil delivery to foodservice kitchens in the state of California, with a wide variety of both non-GMO and natural oils. Its business model is as follows:

1) The company sources different varieties of cooking oil from farmers and stores these in its distribution centre.
2) Clients register and place orders of cooking oils from its website.
3) The company delivers the cooking oils to clients.
4) The company then replaces and collects used cooking oils from the kitchens of clients and disposes the cooking oil sustainably.

The company's oil distribution program is a labour of love created as a response to California Recycle's vision 'to inspire and challenge Californians to achieve the highest waste reduction, recycling, and reuse goals in the nation through innovation and creativity, sound advancement in science and technology, and efficient programs that improve economic vitality and environmental sustainability'.

Not one to shy away from a challenge, ERS is pioneering innovative foodservice systems to support waste reduction and restore our delicate eco-system with our progressive program partners. Its vision is to progress the green initiative in the foodservice industry through education and environmentally sound programme implementation.

Bernadette also says, 'As current legislation and consumer interest indicates, the future of all food storage and packaging will be green. ERS will continue to pave the way for modern, sustainable packaging, distribution, and disposal in the foodservice industry. That means putting our beliefs into action; from start to finish, we work hard to improve the environment through our products, services, and the very structure of our company. We build personal, lasting relationships with our partners, educating them on green alternatives and how decreasing their carbon footprint now will positively impact their business and the planet in the future.'

Questions

1) The company is now considering expanding its customer base by entering and serving the business-to-consumer market with the aim of educating and providing its products and services to this new segment. Using the DODCAR framework, prepare a report explaining the market research process that the company can adopt to identify and serve the needs of potential business-to-consumers clients.

2) Propose a new business model that the company can adopt and implement to serve this new segment.

CHAPTER SIX

Market Segmentation, Targeting and Positioning

Segmentation implies dividing the total market into identifiable subgroups with similar characteristics and then devoting organizational resources to satisfy the needs of these subgroups. The aim of segmentation is to help the organization to differentiate its product offerings to different groups of customers.

The era of mass marketing is ending as more and more companies are adopting and practising segmentation to better address the needs of customers. 'Big data' is enabling firms to build more detailed models of consumer behaviour. Big data capitalizes on developing market trends to allow businesses to become far more specific when segmenting their customers.

One of the big trends in market segmentation is predictive modelling. This involves looking at a consumer's past behaviour to assess how she or he will act in the future. These models use variable factors likely to influence future behaviour or results – gender, age, purchase history and so on. For example, predictive modelling can help in determining which customers are most likely to renew a subscription, for example. With this information, special retention offers can be extended only to those customers most likely to cancel. In predictive modelling, a model is developed, predictions are made and the model is validated or revised as further information becomes available. It also involves using models to find subtle data patterns that answer questions about customers. These models can employ a simple linear equation or involve complex neural networks that are mapped out by sophisticated software.

The benefits of segmentation are the following:

- Better identification and understanding of customer needs. This is because of the intense focus on a distinct segment and with specialization comes expertise.
- Strong brand name in that particular market or industry. Firms that practice segmentation tend to be popular and have a strong brand name in the minds of the segment served.
- Achieving greater market share. This can be explained by the rationale that with a strong brand name and solid understanding of the needs of the segment served. Such segment customers tend to be very loyal, will repeat purchase frequently and will also recommend the product to others.
- Making cross-selling or new product introduction easier and much more readily acceptable. This is particularly the case when the firm is launching new products targeted at the chosen segment. Because they are already loyal customers who trust and value the brand.
- Contributing towards the better utilization and allocation of organizational resources. This implies that the firm will know exactly how best to reach and serve its segment and will devote its resources to serving its customers very efficiently and effectively. For example, the firm will spend its advertising budget on the most appropriate communication channels to reach its segment as opposed to mass advertising.

Criteria for Effective Segmentation

Before the decision is made to segment a particular market, the following segmentation criteria must be fulfilled or satisfied. The criteria for effective segmentation is known as MASH:

M = Measurable – quantifying the number of people in the segment
A = Accessible – firm must have the necessary resources to be capable of reaching and meeting the needs of the segment

S = Substantial – the segment size should be large enough to be profitable

H = Homogeneous – the customers in the target segment must have similar characteristics or attributes

Bases for B2C Segmentation

Consumer markets can be segmented on any or a combination of the following five bases:

1) **Demographic segmentation** divides the total consumer market based on such factors as:
   - Age
   - Gender
   - Education level
   - Income
   - Occupation
   - Nationality

2) **Geographic segmentation** divides the total market based on the physical location of customers such as:
   - Neighbourhoods
   - Towns
   - Cities
   - Regions
   - Sub-regions
   - Countries
   - Continents

3) **Psychographic segmentation** classifies people in terms of:
   - Lifestyles
   - Values
   - Opinions
   - Personality characteristics
   - Interests

4) **Behavioural segmentation** involves dividing the total market based on the behaviours of consumers. For example, how sensitive is the consumer to marketing mix factors such as price, product quality, place and promotion? This could be based on such attributes as brand loyalty, purchase occasion or quantities of the product bought.

5) **Geo-demographic segmentation** is a segmentation technique that classifies people according to where they live. The idea is based on the assumption that people who live within a particular neighbourhood exhibit similar purchasing behaviours. This system allows organizations to profile the users or potential users of a product or service and then proceed to target customers who match these profiles. ACORN (A Classification of Residential Neighbourhoods) is mostly used in the practice of geo-demographic segmentation. This gives insights about the characteristics of people living in a particular neighbourhood. For example, people living in Hollywood are considered to be wealthy with high levels of disposable income and to be mainly working in the entertainment industry.

Bases for B2B Segmentation

Industrial markets can be segmented on any or a combination of the following bases:

- Location – such as cities, regions, countries, sub-regions or continents
- Size – the relative size of the industry
- Industry – implies that the firm focuses on specific industries such as banking or education
- Size of purchase – volumes or quantities bought by customers (heavy, moderate or light users)
- Income levels – based on the levels of incomes generated by the business segment

The Segmentation Process

Developing and implementing market segmentation involves a number of steps:

1) **Identifying and defining the overall market** – Before getting too deep into segmenting, the first step is to clearly define the overall market. A market that is too broadly defined will not produce meaningful segments.

2) **Identifying potential market segments** – Each market segment needs to have at least one factor that binds it together while separating it from other groups. With that in mind, there are many ways to go about breaking up a market. These could be based on any of the previously explained bases for segmentation such as demographic, geographic, psychographic or behavioural in the case of B2C segmentation.

3) **Evaluating the identified segments** – Once the firm has identified potential market segments, the next step is to evaluate them against MASH criteria to determine if the segments make sense for the firm and offer a real economic opportunity.

4) **Developing segment profiles** – Once the identified segments have been evaluated, the next step is to start developing segment profiles, or detailed descriptions of the market segments across a range of factors and measures. The goal is to describe the consumers in each segment to understand their needs, especially in terms of how distinct they are from other market segments. Segment profiles should provide your company with a deep understanding of the potential consumers within each segment for comparison and strategy purposes. The segment profile should outline important aspects of consumer behaviour, such as consumer needs, brand preferences, product usage levels and price sensitivity. It should also provide a demographic and psychographic description of the segment.

5) **Evaluating segment attractiveness** – With the segment profiles determined, the next step is to start identifying the most attractive

segments for your business. An attractive segment offers solid current and/or long-term profit potential. The firms will at this stage want to evaluate the segments according to a variety of criteria:

- Competitors: How much competition will your firm face for serving this segment and is the firm better or does it enjoy a competitive advantage over its competitors?
- Company resources: Does the firm have the right strengths to compete in this segment?
- Segment size: Does this segment offer enough potential sales?
- Segment growth rate: Is the segment growing or shrinking? What is its future?
- Segment profitability: Does this segment have a high or low profit margin?
- Segment accessibility: Can the firm reach the segment through clear communication and distribution channels?
- Segment differentiation: Is the segment distinct enough that it will respond to product and service offerings differently than other groups?

6) **Selecting target segments** – At this stage, the firm should now have enough information to select one or more market segments that fit with the firm's strategy and offer good potential for growth.

Targeting

Targeting involves making the decision about which market segments a firm decides to prioritize for its sales and marketing efforts. Once target segments are identified, the marketing manager selects a targeting strategy that will be the best fit for reaching them. Targeted marketing enables the marketing and sales teams to customize their message to the targeted group(s) of consumers in a focused manner.

The targeting strategy is where the marketing mix comes together to create the right offer and marketing approach for each target segment. Market segments can be targeted using any of the following strategies:

1) **Undifferentiated / Mass targeting** involves marketing to the entire market in the same way. Mass marketing effectively ignores segmentation and instead generates a single offer and marketing mix for everyone. The market is treated as a homogeneous aggregate. Mass marketing aims to reach the largest audience possible, and exposure to the product is maximized. In theory, this directly correlates with a larger number of sales or buy-in to the product.

   Mass marketing tries to spread a marketing message to anyone and everyone willing to listen. Communication tends to be less personal, as evidenced by common mass-marketing tactics: national television, radio and print advertising campaigns; nationally focused coupons; nationally focused point-of-purchase displays. The success of mass marketing depends on whether it is possible to reach enough people, through mass-communication techniques and one universal product offer, to keep them interested in the product and make the strategy worthwhile. While mass-marketing tactics tend to be costly because they operate on a large scale, this approach yields efficiencies and cost savings for companies because it requires the marketing team to execute only one product offer and marketing mix.

   For certain types of widely consumed items (e.g., gasoline, soft drinks, white bread), the undifferentiated market approach makes the most sense. For example, toothpaste is not made specifically for one consumer segment, and it is sold in huge quantities. The manufacturer's goal is to get more people to select and buy their particular brand – Crest, say – over another when they come to the point of purchase. Many mass-marketed products are considered a staple or everyday product. People buy new ones when the old ones wear out or are used up and mass-marketed brand loyalty might be the primary driver when they decide which replacement product to purchase.

2) **Differentiated targeting** is one in which the company decides to provide separate offerings to each different market segment that it

targets. It is also referred to as multi-segment marketing. Each segment is targeted in a particular way, as the company provides unique benefits to different segments. The goal is to help the company increase sales and market share across each segment it targets. Proctor and Gamble, for example, segments some of its markets by gender, and it has separate product offerings and marketing plans for each: the Secret-brand deodorant for women, and Rogaine (a treatment for hair loss) for men.

When it is successful, differentiated marketing can create a very strong, entrenched market presence that is difficult for competitors to displace because of consumers' strong affinity for products and offers that meet the unique needs of their segment. A differentiated strategy can be a smart approach for new companies entering a market, to lure customers away from established players and capture share in a large overall market. Often, established companies become vulnerable to new competitors because they do not give sufficient attention to the perfect marketing mix for any given market segment.

However, differentiated marketing is also very expensive. It carries higher costs for the company because it requires the development of unique products to fit each target segment. Likewise, each unique product and market segment requires its own marketing plans and execution: unique messages, campaigns and promotional tactics and investments. Costs can add up quickly, especially if you are targeting many unique market segments.

For a large company such as Kraft, the cost of this kind of marketing is well worth it, since its products are sold all over the world. An example of its differentiated marketing strategy are the many surprising variations of the famous Oreo cookie developed for the Chinese market. Consumers there can enjoy Oreos with cream flavours such as green-tea ice cream, raspberry–blueberry, mango-orange and grape–peach. All of these Oreo formulations have been heavily market tested and are based on the unique preferences of Chinese consumers.

3) **Concentrated targeting / Niche marketing** is a strategy that targets only one or a few very defined and specific segments of the consumer

population. The goal is to achieve high penetration among the narrowly defined target segments. For example, the manufacturer of Rolex watches has chosen to concentrate on only the luxury segment of the watch market.

An organization that adopts a niche strategy gains an advantage by focusing all efforts on only one or a small handful of segments. All of their market analysis, product development, marketing strategy and tactics concentrate on serving that select part of the market. When they do it well, this approach can provide a differential advantage over other organizations that do not concentrate all their efforts on the 'niche' segment(s). Niche targeting is particularly effective for small companies with limited resources, as it does not require the use of mass production, mass distribution or mass advertising. When a company is highly successful in desirable 'niche' market segments, it can be very profitable.

The primary disadvantage of niche marketing is that it makes companies vulnerable to demand in the narrow market segments they serve. As long as demand is robust, the organization's financial position will be strong. However, if something changes and demand drops off, the company has nothing to cushion it from financial hardship. Since the company has focused all efforts on one market (essentially risking everything on one endeavour), the firm is always somewhat at risk. Such companies are especially vulnerable to small shifts in population or consumer tastes, which can greatly affect their position (for better or for worse). Large competitors with deeper pockets may choose to enter a market and use their size and resources to put smaller, niche players out of business. To insulate themselves from this type of risk, many companies pursing a niche strategy may target multiple segments.

Luxury-goods providers are a great illustration of the challenges of the niche marketing strategy. When economic recessions occur, luxury-goods providers like Rolex, Chanel and Armani routinely struggle financially because their narrow segment of luxury consumers has less disposable income. When fickle consumer tastes shift from Ralph Lauren to Dolce & Gabbana to Prada (and back again), the company's profitability can be uncertain.

4) **Micromarketing or Customized targeting** is a targeting strategy that focuses even more narrowly than niche marketing. It caters to the needs of individuals ('individual marketing') or very small segments in a targeted geography ('local marketing'). Micromarketing can be very powerful by giving consumers exactly what they want, when they want it. However, to achieve large-scale success with this approach, companies must figure out how to meet highly individualized needs efficiently and profitably.

Individual marketing is sometimes referred to as 'customization' or 'one-to-one marketing'. With this approach, companies offer consumers a product created to their individual specifications. For example, Build-A-Bear Workshop invites children to create their own custom stuffed animals. A child can select the type of animal, from teddy bear to unicorn, along with colour, size, clothing and other accessories. Creators of handmade goods on Etsy.com take orders from buyers who may request variations on the individually crafted jewelry, clothing, toys and other items displayed on the website.

Achieving wide-scale success with individual marketing requires product providers to develop production strategies and an entire marketing mix that can ramp up as demand grows. Frequently this involves offering a baseline product with parameters that customers can customize to fit their needs. The advent of digital print technologies has also made mass customization a viable targeting strategy for companies like Vistaprint and Sticker Mule. They provide custom print materials, stickers, decals and other printed products for businesses and individuals using designs created and uploaded by customers. Their primary messaging emphasizes custom products designed by and for individual customers, matching their unique needs and preferences.

Local marketing is a targeting strategy focused expressly on a small, clearly defined neighbourhood or geographic area. Organizations using this technique strive to generate a strong local presence, and targets may include any person or organization within that small area. Groupon and Amazon Local are excellent examples of local marketing. Both online services collaborate with local businesses to promote timely offers and special pricing for individuals living in a designated geographic area. Limited-time and limited-quantity deals may include restaurant meals, spa treatments, performances, recreational activities, lessons and hotel accommodations, along with a wide variety of other local area products and services. These local marketing companies earn revenue when consumers purchase and redeem the special offers in their neighbourhood or city. Another example are farm cooperatives and CSAs (community-supported agriculture shares), which virtually always use a local marketing strategy. They market locally grown produce and farm-fresh goods to people living in the immediate community, and their ongoing goal is to increase local supply and demand for healthy, local, farm-fresh food and produce.

These different targeting strategies are illustrated in the diagram below.

Market Targeting Strategies

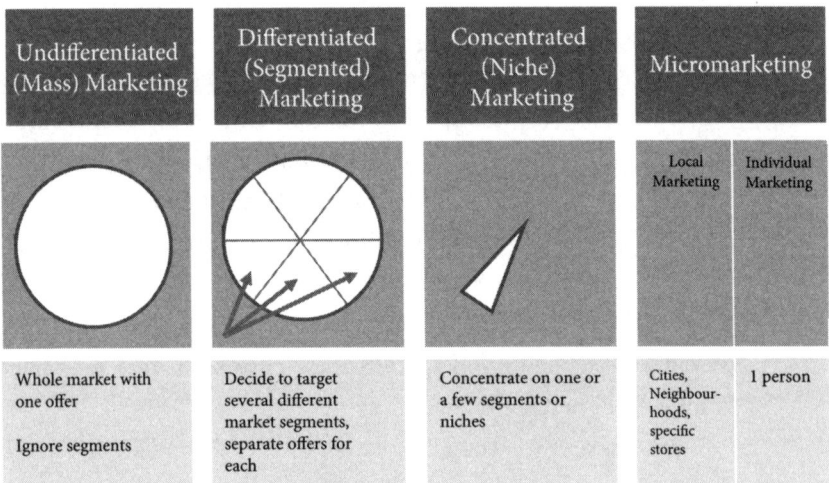

Figure 8: Types of Targeting Strategies

Applying the Marketing Mix to Support Targeting Strategy

Once the firm has chosen its targeting strategy, it must then decide on how best to serve the chosen target market through the application of the marketing mix – namely product, price, place and promotion.

Marketing Mix Element	Targeting Criteria
Product	What would make the ideal product for your target segment?
	What special features or capabilities are critical for this segment?
	What unique problems does your product help this segment solve?
Promotion	What are the best ways to get your target segment's attention?
	What do you want this segment to remember about your product?
Place / Distribution	Where does this segment look or shop for your product?
	What is the best way to get your product to your target customers?
Price	What price(s) are your target customers willing to pay for your product?
	How much is too expensive? How much is too cheap?

Positioning

Positioning relates to how the firm's products are perceived by consumers relative to competitors. In other words, what comes to consumers' minds when the firms' products and/or services are mentioned? The objective of market positioning is to establish the image or identity of a brand or product so that consumers perceive it in a certain way.

Firms can position their products to consumers by any of the following positioning strategies:

- Product use – Advil for easing pain
- Product user – Gatorade for athletes
- Price and quality – Ryanair for low prices and basic flights
- Product feature – Apple iPhone with Siri
- Product class – Louis Vuitton for luxury
- Competitor – Apple and Samsung in the mobile phone market
- Benefit – Volvo for safety
- Cultural symbol – Italian pasta, Russian vodka, German engineering

Process of Developing a Positioning Strategy

There are four distinct steps to adopt and apply when developing a positioning strategy:

1) **Determine company uniqueness by comparing it to competitors** – compare and contrast differences between your company and competitors to identify opportunities. Focus on the firm's strengths but also consider how the firm can exploit these opportunities.

2) **Identify current market position** – determine both the firm's current or existing market position and how the planned new positioning will set the firm apart from competitors.

3) **Competitor position analysis** – identify the marketplace conditions and the amount of influence each competitor can have on each other.

4) **Develop a positioning strategy** – after achieving an understanding, via the preceding steps, of what your company is, how your company is different from competitors, the conditions of the marketplace and opportunities in the marketplace, you can determine how to position the company.

Product/Market Repositioning

Product/market repositioning is when a company changes its existing brand or product status in the marketplace. Repositioning is usually done in response to declining performance or major shifts in the environment. Many companies, however, avoid repositioning and instead choose to launch a new product or brand because of the high cost and effort required to successfully reposition a brand or product.

The Coca-Cola Company launched Mother Energy Drinks in 2006 into the Australian market. The launch campaign was well executed and Coca-Cola was able to leverage its distribution channels to get the product into major retailers. However, the taste of Mother Energy Drink was subpar and repeat purchases were very low. Coca-Cola was faced with a decision: to improve and reposition the product or withdraw it and introduce a new brand and product. The company ultimately decided to reposition the product due to already high brand awareness. The biggest challenge faced by Coca-Cola was to persuade consumers to try the product again. The company changed the packaging, increased the size of the can and improved the taste of the product. The relaunch of the product featured a new phrase – 'New Mother, tastes nothing like the old one.' Ultimately, Coca-Cola was able to successfully reposition Mother Energy Drinks and the brand today competes with the two leading energy drinks in the market: V and Red Bull.

PlaceMe Living: Reshaping the Real Estate Residential Market

Company background

Founded in 2016, PlaceMe is the brainchild of Clara Arroyave, who found an opportunity to launch the company based on her own personal experiences whilst studying and living in Boston, USA. Clara was an international student from Colombia who came to Boston to study on an MBA program. On arriving in Boston, she found it very hard to lease an apartment in the city, mainly because property owners or property management agencies were asking for a social security number as well as credit scores, which she did not have considering that she was new to both the country and the city. Additionally, social security applications were taking at least two weeks to process and one had to live in the US for some six months before qualifying for a credit score report. She also found that international students and young professionals coming into the city from overseas did not have a good understanding of the rental market in the US, paid extra fees, bought furniture that they were not able to sell after their time in the city, and often lived in locations with poor access to public transportation.

Business Model

Based on her experiences, Clara came up with the idea to launch a company that would make it more convenient for people like her to be able to rent properties in Boston, and PlaceMe was born in November 2016. The company exists to simplify the rental market for young professionals and students by leasing fully-furnished bedrooms at a flat monthly rent and with flexible lease terms. Over 80 per cent of PlaceMe tenants are international newcomers and appreciate the no-haggle, no-hassle lease options provided by the company.

Through its platform, the company provides a carefully selected portfolio of exclusive properties with three to four bedrooms in each property. Tenants pay a flat fee that includes a furnished bedroom, utilities such as cable television and Internet, and also cleaning. Occupancy rates currently stand at 97 per cent and gender distribution is 73 per cent male and 27 per cent female as at September 2019. Its tenants can be students studying at the local colleges or professionals working in industry in the city of Boston, who share an apartment with each having their own bedroom.

The company positions itself as having sound understanding and appreciation of knowing what it is like to be a newcomer in a new city. PlaceMe is about family: creating memories and building lifelong friendships.

The company's stated vision is: 'Our vision is to promote the benefits of the co-living environment. One that creates improved efficiency in housing while also helping to build strong relationships between students and professionals from around the world.'

The City of Boston

There are 114 higher education institutions in Massachusetts, according to the Carnegie Classification of Institutions of Higher Education. More than 50 of those are in the greater Boston metropolitan area, which is home to more than 350,000 students. These institutions include state universities such as the University of Massachusetts, private universities such as Harvard, Hult International Business School and MIT, as well as local colleges. The higher education industry accounts for more than 165,000 jobs and nearly US$11 billion in revenue in metro Boston, according to data from Emsi, a labour-market data firm.

However, even those figures vastly understate its importance to the economy. Higher education is the foundation that supports even larger Boston-based industries, including healthcare and tech. Then there are the students themselves: pouring money into the local economy through everything from off-campus rentals to concert tickets.

The state of Massachusetts is also home to many large corporations such as Liberty Mutual, State Street, Fidelity Investments, Staples and Boston Consulting Group, among many others, as well as being home to a thriving start-up community. Boston is the fifth-best city in the world for technology start-ups, according to a recent report from research group and accelerator start-up Genome. In December 2019 alone, 41 start-ups raised more than US$920 million. This number might not surprise some, considering the city is home to an emerging talent pool of graduates from eminent educational institutions, accelerators like Techstars and Mass Challenge, and major tech companies (including Facebook) building second outposts and creating new jobs.

The Rental Market in Pandemic Times

Due to the prevailing pandemic situation, the rental market in many places including Boston was almost unrecognizable by the beginning of 2021: vacant apartments abounded, rents were dropping, and property owners were willing to waive fees, allow pets, grant lease flexibility and do pretty much anything to secure a paying tenant.

A recent report from Zumper shows that one-bedroom rents in Boston had a 6 per cent year-on-year decrease in 2020, a decline the city had not seen since 2016. It is yet another symptom of the pandemic: San Francisco and New York, the other top rental markets in the USA, followed suit with reductions of 11 per cent and 7 per cent respectively. As for inventory, 'when comparing available one-bedroom Boston listings in July 2019 to July 2020, the number of available units has doubled', says Crystal Chen, an analyst at Zumper. To put it plainly:

there are more units than interested tenants, and the traditional power dynamic has flipped.

Beyond lower rates, property owners are piling on other incentives to sweeten the pot and lure occupants inside. John Puma, COO of Boston-based real estate agency and apartment listing site Places for Less, has been keeping a close eye on the rental market. He has seen market-rate apartments offering a month of free rent, with luxury buildings shelling out two or even three gratis months in some cases. 'They'd rather take a reduced rent for the remainder of the year than have it go vacant for who knows how long,' he explains. He has seen property manager flexibility extend to credit scores, income bracket and even employment status: 'Landlords have accepted tenants based on just their unemployment income right now.' In addition, for local and international students who are sticking around the city, some property owners are forgoing the usual requirement for a co-signer (or guarantor), a time-honoured hindrance for students seeking housing in Boston. Other housing providers are paying the broker's fees themselves, waiving security deposits, and accommodating month-to-month or semester-long leases. It is the renter's market that, in some ways, has always been needed, but never actually arrived – if only it had not taken a global pandemic to bring it about.

Question

Based on the information given in this case study, identify and explain the segmentation, targeting and positioning strategies that PlaceMe could consider adopting.

CHAPTER SEVEN

The Marketing Mix

The practice of marketing revolves around the adoption and application of the marketing mix. This is the heart of marketing, and how it is practised can very much determine organizational success or otherwise. In its most basic sense, the marketing mix refers to the seven variables (the 7Ps) that we've already mentioned, which are used by marketers in operationalizing their marketing plans, strategies and tactics: Product, Price, Place, Promotion, People, Process and Physical Evidence.

It is imperative that marketers invest time, resources and commitment in delivering each of the seven variables efficiently and effectively. Getting one or more of these variables wrong can have a profound effect on the firm's entire marketing operations.

The Product Mix

A product is anything that is produced to satisfy the needs of consumers. Examples of products include the following:

- Physical goods such as cars
- Services such as banking
- Events such as the Olympics
- Places such as Paris
- People such as Cristiano Ronaldo

One thing that all these examples have in common is that they are produced or promoted by organizations and/or consumed by consumers to meet and satisfy consumer needs accordingly. Some organizations produce both products and services – as is the case with many car manufacturers, which not only manufacture cars but also deliver car maintenance services.

In marketing, the study of the product mix entails:

- New Product Development
- Product Life Cycle (PLC)
- Branding
- Services Marketing
- Packaging

New Product Development

To remain relevant and succeed, firms need to develop and launch new products. This is important for the following number of reasons:

- To address consumers' ever-changing needs
- To replace existing products that are in decline or unprofitable
- To generate new sources of income
- To gain competitive advantage and outperform competitors
- To enhance brand image
- To attract investors and employees

New Product Development Process

The new product development process explains the distinct stages that firms go through when developing new products. These stages include the following:

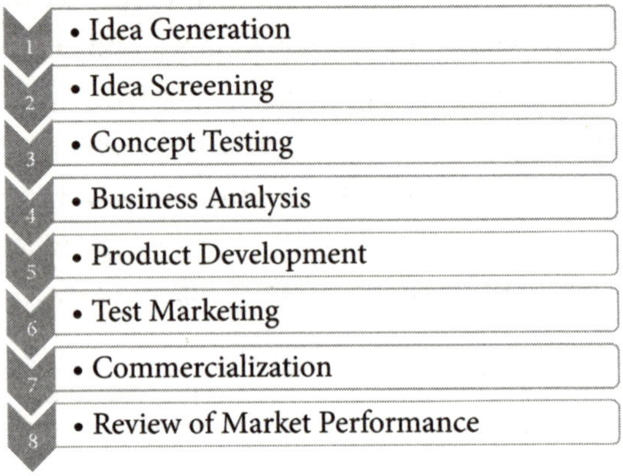

1. • Idea Generation
2. • Idea Screening
3. • Concept Testing
4. • Business Analysis
5. • Product Development
6. • Test Marketing
7. • Commercialization
8. • Review of Market Performance

Figure 9: New Development Process

1) **Idea Generation**

Every product originates from an idea before it is developed and launched into the market. Sources of new product ideas can be obtained from employees, research and development department, competitors, inventors, suppliers, distributors and customers.

2) **Idea Screening**

This stage involves filtering all the ideas generated and then choosing the most workable ones and dropping the others. Developing new products can be extremely expensive, so it is imperative that the firm narrows down and selects only the best ideas based on a consideration of such factors as profitability, the needs of the market and the resources available for production.

3) **Concept Testing**

This stage entails turning the chosen ideas into a product concept, which is a detailed version of the new product-idea stated in more meaningful consumer terms. This detailed version includes concept development and concept testing.

4) **Concept Development**

Imagine a car manufacturer that has developed an all-electric car. The idea has passed the idea screening and must now be developed into a concept. The marketer's task is to develop this new product into alternative product concepts. Then, the company can find out how attractive each concept is to customers and choose the best one. Possible product concepts for this electric car could be:

- A – an affordably priced mid-size car designed as a second family car to be used around town for visiting friends and doing shopping.
- B – a mid-priced sporty compact car appealing to young singles and couples.
- C – a high-end midsize utility vehicle appealing to those who like the space that SUVs provide but who also want an economical car.
- As you can see, these concepts need to be quite precise in order to be meaningful. In the next sub-stage, each concept is tested.

5) **Concept Testing**

New product concepts need to be tested with groups of target consumers. The concepts can be presented to consumers either symbolically or physically. The question is always: does the particular concept have strong consumer appeal? For some concept tests, a word or picture description might be sufficient. However, to increase the reliability of the test, a more concrete and physical presentation of the product concept may be needed. After exposing the concept to the group of target consumers, they will be asked to answer questions in order to find out the consumer appeal and customer value of each concept.

6) **Product Development**

This stage involves the actual development of the idea into a fully functional product, which has moved on from just being a concept. Prototypes of the product are made, there are major and significant increases in production costs and often a lot of time is invested at this stage.

7) **Test Marketing**

Once prototypes are produced, the firm will test the product in real consumer settings with real consumers, who will be given samples of the product to test and then asked for their feedback. Feedback will include a consideration for such issues as quality, price, design, brand name chosen, purchase intentions and product adoption and repurchase intentions.

8) **Commercialization**

Acting on the feedback obtained in the test marketing stage and having made any necessary modifications where necessary, the firm will produce the product in large quantities and launch it in the market so that consumers can actually buy it. This stage is characterized by huge capital investments in distribution, marketing and promotions to create awareness of the existence of the product in the minds of its targeted consumers.

9) **Review of Marketing Performance**

The final stage involves reviewing and measuring the performance of the new product in the market. Marketing performance metrics include sales levels, profit levels, demand levels, market share against competitors, levels of product/brand awareness, relative costs, customer retention levels and the number of repeat purchases.

The Product Life Cycle

Once the product is launched into the market after the commercialization stage, it starts its life cycle. The product life cycle (PLC) identifies and explains the different stages that a product goes through in its lifespan. This is one of the most important concepts in marketing because it enables the marketing team to understand what happens to the product at each stage as well as the potential strategies that can be adopted to manage the product at each stage. How long the product exists in the market and performs in terms of sales and profitability very much depends on how it is managed.

The product life cycle consists of four distinct stages, namely introduction, growth, maturity and decline.

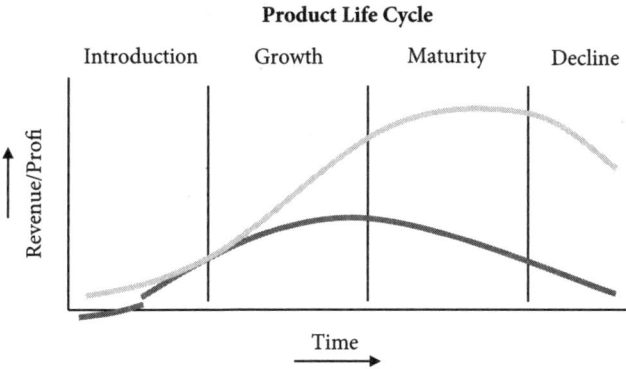

Figure 10: Product Life Cycle

Each of the four stages are explained in terms of what happens at each stage and what strategies the firm can deploy to manage the product at each stage. It is worth emphasizing that the nature of the product and the target audiences makes how each product is managed unique.

1) **Introduction Stage**

   This stage, when the product is new in the market, is characterized by the following factors:
   - Consumer demand is typically low
   - Low levels of sales
   - Profits are not made yet and the product is mostly a loss-maker at this stage
   - Low levels of brand or product awareness
   - Production costs are typically high
   - Initial perceptions of the product

   To overcome these challenges, the efforts of the marketing team should focus on the following strategies:
   - Engage in heavy advertising to create and increase product awareness in the minds of the target audiences

- Offer promotional incentives to drive up demand. Such incentives can include introductory price discounts, BOGOF, free samples, more for less, etc.
- Feedback on consumer perceptions should be factored into the marketing efforts with a view to making any necessary changes

2) **Growth Stage**

This is the second stage of the product life cycle and characterized by the following:

- Sales are picking up as a result of the advertising and promotional initiatives adopted and implemented at the introduction stage
- Strong growth in profits
- Levels of consumer awareness are increasing
- Competitors are likely to enter the market to take advantage of growing sales
- Production costs tend to go down as a result of economies of scale

As a result, the marketing team should consider the following strategies:

- Continue to advertise but with more emphasis on product differentiation from competitors
- Increase prices to denote the quality of the product and also to offset the lower introductory or promotional pricing adopted in the introduction stage
- Adding new features to the product
- Introducing consumer loyalty programmes to minimize switching to competing products

3) **Maturity Stage**

This is the third stage of the product life cycle – and a very critical one, for that matter. This stage is characterized by the following:

- Sales tend to peak at this stage
- Profits are made
- Competition in the market tends to be high
- Consumers have many choices of the product to choose from

The firm can consider adopting a combination of the following strategies:

- Advertise to remind consumers of the product, with an emphasis on differentiating features and product attributes
- Offer promotional incentives to maintain consumer interest and demand
- Add additional features to the products
- Make the distribution of the product more widely available by, for example, entering new markets

4) **Decline Stage**

The last stage of the product life is the decline stage, which does not bode well for any product. Every effort should be made to avoid or delay this stage, which is characterized by the following attributes:

- Sales are falling due to the intensity of competition in the market as well as consumer fatigue
- Profits are going down due to the decrease in sales revenues, and in some cases, losses are incurred
- Product saturation sets in with so many different competing products in the market

At this stage, the firm may consider the following strategies:

- Staying in the market to survive with minimal investments in terms of adding new features, in the expectation that competitors will exit from the market
- Inject investment to add new features that will make the product more appealing
- Cut prices to generate higher sales volumes
- Selective promotion by focusing such promotional efforts on the most likely consumer segments to buy
- Harvest the product – sell it to other firms that may be able to revive its fortunes
- Divest – by withdrawing the product from the market

- Launch the product in other countries or markets where there is demand
- Consider alternative uses for the product with the expectation of prolonging its lifespan

Limitations / Criticisms of the Product Life Cycle

Despite its relative importance, especially in terms of ensuring the existence and performance of the product in the market, the product life cycle has some limitations:

- The different stages of the product life cycle cannot be easily defined due to the interrelated nature of the stages. Where one stage ends or another begins is not clear-cut, and this makes it difficult for managers to develop the best strategies to deal with each stage.
- Not all products follow the logic of the life cycle by going through the different stages in a sequential order. This means that some products are introduced and then go straight to the decline stage.
- The strategies proposed for each of the different stages might not necessarily work as these are also dependent on market conditions especially competitor activities.

Kellogg's Nutri-Grain

Extending the Product Life Cycle

Businesses need to set themselves clear aims and objectives if they are going to succeed. The Kellogg Company is the world's leading producer of breakfast cereals and convenience foods such as cereal bars, and it aims to maintain that position. In 2006, Kellogg's had total worldwide sales of almost $11 billion (£5.5 billion). In 2007, it was Britain's biggest selling grocery brand, with sales of more than £550 million. Product lines include ready-to-eat cereals (i.e. not hot cereals like porridge) and nutritious snacks, such as cereal bars. Kellogg's brands are household names around the world and include Rice Krispies, Special K and Nutri-Grain, while some of its brand characters, like Snap, Crackle and Pop, are among the most well-known in the world.

Kellogg's has achieved this position by offering great brands and great brand value, but also through a strong commitment to corporate social responsibility. All of Kellogg's business aims are set within a particular context or set of ideals. Central to this is Kellogg's passion for the business, the brands and the food, demonstrated through the promotion of healthy living.

The company divides its market into six key segments. Kellogg's Corn Flakes has been on breakfast tables for over 100 years and represents the 'Tasty Start' cereals that people eat to start their day. Other segments include 'Simply Wholesome' products that are good for you, such as Kashi Muesli, 'Shape Management' products, such as Special K, and 'Inner Health' lines, such as All-Bran. Children may be most familiar with the 'Kid Preferred' brands, such as Frosties, while brands like Raisin Wheats are recognized by parents as being better for their children.

Each brand has to hold its own in a competitive market. Brand managers monitor the success of brands in terms of market share, growth and performance against the competition. Key decisions have to be made about the future of any brand that is not succeeding. This case study is about Nutri-Grain. It shows how Kellogg's recognized there was a problem with the brand and used business tools to reach a solution. The overall aim was to relaunch the brand and return it to growth in its market.

Kellogg's and the product life cycle

Each product has its own life cycle. It will be 'born', it will 'develop', it will 'grow old' and, eventually, it will 'die'. Some products, like Kellogg's Corn Flakes, have retained their market position for a long time. Others may have their success undermined by falling market share or by competitors. The product life cycle shows how sales of a product change over time.

The five typical stages of the life cycle are shown on a graph. However, perhaps the most important stage of a product life cycle happens before this graph starts, namely the Research and Development (R&D) stage. Here the company designs a product to meet a need in the market. The costs of market research (to identify a gap in the market) and of product development (to ensure that the product meets the needs of that gap) are called 'sunk' or start-up costs. Nutri-Grain was originally designed to meet the needs of busy people who had missed breakfast. It aimed to provide a healthy cereal breakfast in a portable and convenient format.

1) *Launch.* Many products do well when they are first brought out and Nutri-Grain was no exception. From launch (the first stage on the diagram) in 1997, it was immediately successful, gaining almost 50 per cent share of the growing cereal bar market in just two years.

2) *Growth.* Nutri-Grain's sales steadily increased as the product was promoted and became well known. It maintained growth in sales

until 2002 through expanding the original product with new developments of flavour and format. This is good for the business, as it does not have to spend money on new machines or equipment for production. The market position of *Nutri-Grain* also subtly changed from a 'missed breakfast' product to an 'all-day' healthy snack.

3) *Maturity.* Successful products attract other competitor businesses to start selling similar products. This indicates the third stage of the life cycle – maturity. This is the time of maximum profitability, when profits can be used to continue to build the brand. However, competitor brands from both Kellogg itself (e.g. All-Bran bars) and other manufacturers (e.g. Alpen bars) offered the same benefits, and this slowed down sales and chipped away at Nutri-Grain's market position. Kellogg continued to support the development of the brand, but some products (such as Minis and Twists), struggled in a crowded market. Although Elevenses continued to succeed, this was not enough to offset the overall sales decline.

Not all products follow these stages precisely and periods for each stage will vary widely. Growth, for example, may take place over a few months or, as in the case of Nutri-Grain, over several years.

4) *Decline.* Clearly, at this point, Kellogg had to make a key business decision. Sales were falling; the product was in decline and losing its position. Should Kellogg let the product 'die' – i.e. withdraw it from the market – or should it try to extend its life?

Strategic use of the product life cycle

When a company recognizes that a product has gone into decline or is not performing as well as it should, it has to decide what to do. The decision needs to be made within the context of the overall aims of the business. Kellogg's aims included the development of great brands, great brand value and the promotion of healthy living. Strategically, Kellogg had a strong position in the market for both healthy foods and convenience foods. Nutri-Grain fitted well with its main aims and objectives and therefore was a product and a brand worth rescuing.

Extending the Nutri-Grain cycle – identifying the problem

Kellogg had to decide whether the problem with Nutri-Grain was the market, the product or both. The market had grown by over 15 per cent and competitors' market shares had increased while Nutri-Grain sales in 2003 had declined. The market in terms of customer tastes had also changed – more people missed breakfast and therefore there was an increased need for such a snack product.

The choice of extension strategy was either product development or diversification. Diversification carries much higher costs and risks. Kellogg decided that it needed to focus on changing the product to meet the changing market needs.

Research showed that there were several issues to address:

1) The brand message was not strong enough in the face of competition. Consumers were not impressed enough by the product to choose it over competitors.

2) Some of the other Kellogg products (e.g. Minis) had taken the focus away from the core business.

3) The core products of Nutri-Grain Soft Bake and Elevenses between them represented over 80 per cent of sales but received a small proportion of advertising and promotion budgets.

4) The sales that were achieved were driven by promotional pricing (discounted pricing) rather than the underlying strength of the brand.

Implementing the extension strategy for Nutri-Grain

Having recognized the problems, Kellogg's developed solutions to rebrand and relaunch the product in 2005.

1) Fundamental to the relaunch was the renewal of the brand image. Kellogg's looked at the core features that made the brand different and modelled the new brand image on these. Nutri-Grain is unique because it is the only product of this kind that is baked. This provided two benefits:

- The healthy grains were soft rather than gritty
- The eating experience is closer to the more indulgent foods that people could be eating (cakes and biscuits, for example). The unique selling point – and hence the focus of the brand – needed to be the 'soft bake'.

2) Researchers also found that a key part of the market was a group termed 'realistic snackers'. These people want to snack on healthy foods but still crave a great tasting snack. The relaunched Nutri-Grain product needed to help this key group fulfil both of these desires.

3) Kellogg decided to refocus investment on the core products of Soft Bake Bars and Elevenses because these had maintained their growth (accounting for 61 per cent of Soft Bake Bar sales). Three existing Soft Bake Bar products were improved, three new ranges introduced and poorly performing ranges (such as Minis) were withdrawn.

4) New packaging was introduced to unify the brand image.

5) An improved pricing structure for stores and supermarkets was developed.

Using this information, the relaunch focused on the four parts of the marketing mix:

- Product – improvements to the recipe and a wider range of flavours, repositioning the brand as 'healthy and tasty', not a substitute for a missed breakfast
- Promotion – a new and clearer brand image to cover all the products in the range along with advertising and point-of-sale materials
- Place – better offers and materials to stores that sold the product
- Price – new price levels were agreed that did not rely on promotional pricing. This improved revenue for both Kellogg and the stores.

As a result, Soft Bake Bar year-on-year sales went from a decline to substantial growth, with sales increasing by almost 50 per cent. The Nutri-Grain brand achieved a retail sales growth rate of almost three times that of the market and most importantly, growth was maintained after the initial re-launch.

Conclusion

Successful businesses use all the tools at their disposal to stay at the top of their chosen market. Kellogg was able to use a number of business tools in order to successfully re-launch the *Nutri-Grain* brand. These tools included the product life cycle, Ansoff's matrix (see Chapter 14) and the marketing mix. Such tools are useful when used properly.

Kellogg was able to see that although Nutri-Grain fitted its strategic profile – a healthy, convenient cereal product – it was underperforming in the market. This information was used along with the aims and objectives of the business, to develop a strategy for continuing success. Finally, when Kellogg checked the growth of the relaunched product against its own objectives, it had met all its aims to:

- Reposition the brand through the use of the marketing mix
- Return the brand to growth
- Improve the frequency of purchase
- Introduce new customers to the brand.

Nutri-Grain remains a growing brand and product within the Kellogg product family.

Question

Identify and analyse the marketing actions undertaken by Kellogg's to manage the product at every stage of the life cycle. What additional recommendations will you suggest to better market the product?

CHAPTER EIGHT

Services Marketing

It is safe to state that in many countries today, services contribute more to gross domestic product (GDP) than manufacturing, especially in such countries as the UK, France and Holland. These countries are characterized by service-based economies, meaning that services contribute significantly more than manufacturing to the creation of wealth. It can be also stated that all industries including manufacturing do involve some aspects of service. The main difference is the extent to which services form an integral part of the firm's activities. The services industry is rapidly growing and includes such sectors as airlines, hotels, banking, finance, consulting and education. This growth in the service sector can be attributed to the following factors:

- The knowledge-based industries such as information technology and consultancy services are experiencing growth and generating huge employment opportunities
- The rapid rise of the entrepreneurial culture, with more people now starting their own enterprises within the services sector
- The explosion in the practice of outsourcing, with more firms now using the services of external providers as a means to cut costs and boost efficiencies
- Pressures on work/life balance imply that more people are now, more than ever before, placing a high importance on spending more of their times on leisure activities. This therefore necessitates more firms providing such leisure activities as travel and holidays

- Many products now include a service component. For example, Apple does not only manufacture high-quality phones but also include high levels of services. Firms use the aftersales services as a basis for competitive differentiation.

In marketing, a service can be defined as any activity of benefit, offered by one party to another, which is intangible and does not result in the ownership of anything. The nature of services make them very difficult to market as compared to physical goods. The nature of services is best explained by identifying and analysing the characteristics of services. These help in explaining and understanding the differences between services and physical goods. There are five characteristics of services:

1) Intangibility
2) Perishability
3) Inseparability
4) Variability or heterogeneity
5) Ownership

Each of these five characteristics of services poses risks or challenges for marketers as well as consumers. Therefore, the emphasis should be on understanding these inherent challenges and, more importantly, devising strategies that will help in overcoming the relative challenges that go together with these characteristics.

Intangibility

This characteristic of service implies that services cannot, by their very nature, be touched or seen. The level of intangibility also varies from one service to another. The challenge is that consumers do not like to buy things that they cannot see or touch. Services by nature have to be purchased before being consumed. Consumers cannot evaluate services prior to consuming the service. For example, food served in restaurants must be consumed before the consumer can assess whether it is good or not.

Therefore, to overcome this challenge or risk, marketers can adopt the following strategies:

- Emphasize the benefits of the service to consumers and not the service itself. This is because consumers do not necessarily buy the service but rather the benefit that comes with the service. For example, a bank can emphasize the benefit of opening an account and not the account itself – the benefits being earning interest, security, as well as easy access.
- Provide testimonials from current or previous consumers. Online reviews are strongly used by hotels, for example, to promote their services.
- Increase the level of tangibility through brochures and other promotional material.

Perishability

This characteristic of services implies that services cannot be stored for future use. Instead, services have to be consumed at set times, otherwise the customer will lose it. Services are therefore dependent on both time and place. This has implications for both consumers and firms. For the consumer, it implies that booking a flight, for example, means flying at a set date, time and place, and consumers cannot change these without at least incurring penalties.

For marketers of services, the following strategies can be considered in mitigating the risk posed by the perishability of services.

- Demand forecasting is critical to manage any excess capacities.
- The firm can offer promotional incentives to encourage consumer demand for services as yet unsold. For example, price discounts can be offered to consumers to encourage uptake of the service.
- Differential pricing can be adopted, whereby different prices are changed at different times to offset lean demand periods.
- Consumers can be encouraged to reserve the service so that demand can be better projected.

- Complementary services can be offered to encourage consumers to use the actual services. For example, some airlines offer free transportation from the airport to consumers' destinations.
- Employees can be employed part-time, depending on the nature of the service to ensure that employees are hired at peak periods. This is prevalent in the hotel and hospitality industry.

Inseparability

This characteristic of services implies that unlike manufacturers of physical goods, service providers cannot be separated from the service provided. In fact, they are a critical part of the service delivery process because services are by nature typically produced and consumed simultaneously. This is not true of physical goods which are manufactured, put into inventory, distributed and consumed later. In the case of services, both the service provider and consumer are involved in the service delivery and consumption process.

- The implication for service providers – and marketers, for that matter – is to ensure that the service is delivered right the first time every time.

Variability/Heterogeneity

This characteristic of services implies that service standards do vary, unlike physical goods, and are inconsistent in terms of their delivery. This can be attributed to the fact that services are in most cases provided and delivered by humans and so suffer from inconsistencies. Human beings are never the same all the time and have mood swings, which can affect the quality of service delivered to consumers.

To minimize the risk associated with service inconsistencies, marketers can employ the following actions:

- Invest in hiring and training procedures to recruit the best employees
- Standardize service delivery processes
- Ensure consistency of quality control procedures
- Monitor customer satisfaction consistently

- Provide employee motivational incentives
- Deploy technology to replace humans in the service delivery processes

Ownership

Unlike physical goods, which are purchased and owned by consumers, the consumers do not own services. The ownership of services belongs to the service provider. A bank account in a customer's name does not necessarily imply that the customer owns the account. However, consumers always like to believe that they own the service.

To mitigate this risk, marketers can take the following actions:

- Allow consumers to continue to believe that they own the service. Provide physical aspects of the service in the customer's name. For example, a bank will provide cards, chequebooks and personal identification numbers as well as statements in the customer's name to encourage them to believe that they own the account.

Managing Service Quality

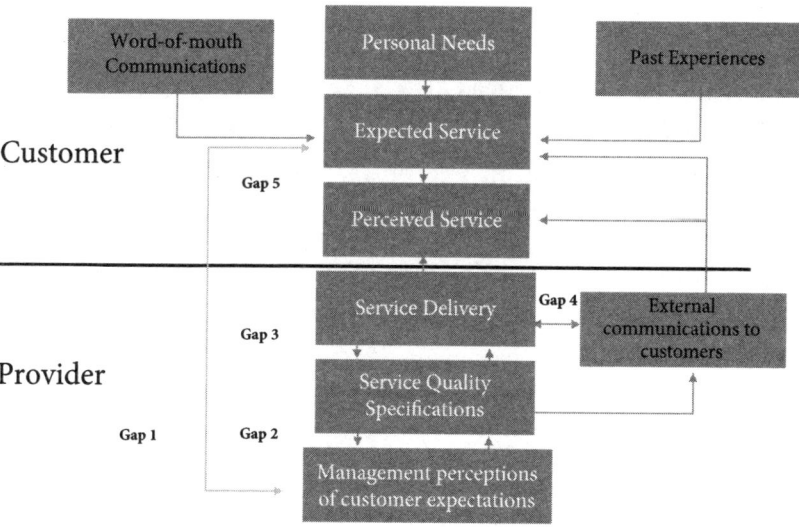

Figure 11: Service Quality Gaps Model

Reasons for Service Quality Gaps

- Gap 1 – Not knowing what customers expect
- Gap 2 – Setting the wrong service quality standards
- Gap 3 – The service performance gap
- Gap 4 – When promises do not match actual delivery
- Gap 5 – The difference between customer perception and expectation

Managing Service Quality for Gap 1 – between consumer expectation and management perception

This gap arises when the management does not correctly perceive what the customers want. For instance, hospital administrators may think patients want better food, but patients may be more concerned with the responsiveness of the nurse.

Key factors leading to this gap are:

- Insufficient marketing research
- Poorly interpreted information about the audience's expectations
- Too many layers between front-line personnel and top-level management

Managing Service Quality for Gap 2 – between management perception and service quality specification

Here the management might correctly perceive what the customer wants but may not set an appropriate performance standard. An example here would be that hospital administrators may tell the nurse to respond to a request quickly, but they may not specify *how* quickly.

Gap 2 may occur for the following reasons:

- Insufficient planning procedures
- Lack of management commitment
- Unclear or ambiguous service design
- Unsystematic new service development process

Managing Service Quality for Gap 3 – between service
quality specification and service delivery

This gap may arise owing to the service personnel. The reasons for this
gap are poor training, incapability or unwillingness to meet the set
service standards. The possible major reasons for this gap are:

- Deficiencies in human resource policies, such as ineffective recruitment,
  role ambiguity, role conflict, improper evaluation and compensation
  system
- Ineffective internal marketing
- Failure to match demand and supply
- Lack of proper customer education and training

Managing Service Quality for Gap 4 – between service delivery and
external communication

Consumer expectations are highly influenced by statements made
by company representatives and advertisements. The gap arises
when these assumed expectations are not fulfilled at the time of
delivery of the service. For example, the brochure may show a
hospital with clean and furnished rooms, but in reality these may
be poorly maintained – in this case the patient's expectations are
not met.

The discrepancy between the actual service and the promised one
may occur due to the following reasons:

- Overpromising in external communication campaign
- Failure to manage customer expectations
- Failure to perform according to specifications

Managing Service Quality for Gap 5 – between expected service
and experienced service

This gap arises when the consumer misinterprets the service quality.
For example, the physician may keep visiting the patient to show and

ensure care, but the patient may interpret this as an indication that something is wrong.

Customer Defection Management

Businesses commonly lose between 15–20 per cent of customers each year. Some services, however, are much higher than this – cable TV is over 50 per cent and mobile phones experience a churn rate of 45 per cent. There are different types of defectors and many reasons why customers defect to other competing brands, such as the following.

- Price defectors – customers buying competing products that are priced lower
- Product defectors – customers switching to other service providers because of dissatisfaction with the product
- Service defectors – customers switching to competitors because of lower than expected service standards and provisions
- Market defectors – customers exiting the market for the product altogether
- Technological defectors – customers stop buying the products because it's not technologically sophisticated or advanced to keep up with their current requirements

Customer Defection Management Process

- **Step 1.** Measurement of customer retention – determination of the percentage of the customer population that the firm is able to retain
- **Step 2.** Identification of the cause of defection and key service issues – identification of the reasons that make customer not to return for repeat purchases
- **Step 3.** Corrective action to improve retention – adoption of the appropriate actions to regain and retain previous and existing customers respectively.

Customers as Contributors to Service Quality, Value and Satisfaction

Customers contribute to service quality when:

- They ask questions
- They take responsibility for their own satisfaction
- They complain! Complaints should be considered as 'opportunities for improvements'

Monitoring and Evaluating Service Delivery

- Customer satisfaction surveys
- Evaluating dissatisfaction
- Performance appraisals
- Employee group discussions
- Mystery shopper experience
- Observing customers receiving service

JetBlue Airways

While this particular case study dates back to 2007–8, the business lessons it illustrates are as valid today as they were at the time.

At the age of 25, entrepreneur David Neeleman co-founded Morris Air, a charter air service that was purchased in 1993 by Southwest Airlines (SWA). Morris Air was a low-fare airline, which pioneered many cost-saving practices that later became standard in the industry. After working as an airline executive for SWA, Neeleman founded another airline, JetBlue Airways, in 1998. When Neeleman established JetBlue, his strategy was to provide air travel at even lower costs than SWA. At the same time, he wanted to offer better service and more amenities.

JetBlue copied and improved upon many of SWA's cost-reducing activities. For example, it started out by using just one type of airplane (the Airbus A320) to lower the costs of aircraft maintenance and pilot training. It also chose to fly point to point, directly connecting highly trafficked city pairs. In contrast, legacy airlines such as Delta, United or American use a hub-and-spoke system; such systems connect many different locations via layovers at airport hubs. The point-to-point business model focuses on directly connecting fewer but more highly trafficked city pairs. The point-to-point system lowers costs by not offering baggage transfers and schedule coordination with other airlines. In addition, JetBlue flew longer distances and transported more passengers per flight than SWA, further driving down its costs. Initially, JetBlue enjoyed the lowest cost per available seat-mile (an important performance metric in the airline industry) in the United States.

At the same time, JetBlue also attempted to enhance its differential appeal by driving up its perceived value. Its intent was to combine high-touch (to enhance the customer experience) and high-tech (to drive down costs). Some of JetBlue's value-enhancing features included high-end 100-seat Embraer regional jets with leather seats, individual TV screens with popular film and television programming, 100 channels of XM Satellite Radio and free in-flight Wi-Fi capabilities, along with friendly and attentive on-board service and other amenities. Also, despite a highly functional website for reservations and other travel-related services, JetBlue recognized that one-third of customers prefer speaking to a live reservation agent, and decided to employ stay-at-home parents in the United States instead of following industry best practice by outsourcing its reservation system to India. The company suggests this 'home sourcing' is more productive than outsourcing; it also says that customers' appreciation of the reservation experience more than makes up for the wage differential between the United States and India. To sum it up, JetBlue's 'Customer Bill of Rights' declared its dedication to 'bringing humanity back to air travel'.

In early 2007, however, JetBlue's reputation for outstanding customer service took a major hit: several flights were delayed due to a snowstorm in which the airline kept passengers on board the aircraft; some sat on the tarmac for up to nine hours. Many wondered whether JetBlue was losing its magic touch. In May 2007, David Neeleman left JetBlue. Ever the entrepreneur, he went on to found Azul Brazilian Airlines in 2008.

Question

Based on the information provided in the case study, what actions do you think the post-Neeleman management of JetBlue could have done to recover from its crisis in service provision?

CHAPTER NINE

Brand Management

A brand is an organization's most important asset and so requires careful management. A brand can be defined in the simplest terms as a name, sign, symbol, logo or slogan that identifies and differentiates the organization from competitors, and may identify one product item or a whole family of product items.

However, it is worth noting that brands which transcend the physical level to reach the emotional level are extremely powerful. This implies that consumers do not buy a brand for only its physical attributes or characteristics but also for the emotional benefits that the brand conveys to consumers. For example, Harley Davidson is not marketed simply as a motorbike; more importantly, perhaps, it is a bike that makes riders feel independent, free and rebellious.

Brand Elements

The essence of a strong brand is to be sufficiently differentiated that its competitors cannot easily replicate it. This level of differentiation implies that a brand has many distinctive characteristics, and to achieve this, it is important to understand how brands are constructed.

Brands consist of two major types of attributes, namely:

1) Emotional or Intrinsic
2) Functional or Extrinsic

Functional and Emotional Aspects of Branding

Functional	Emotional
'What the product does' ... performance	'What the brand means' ... image
Objective, rational, tangible	Subjective, 'perceptions', intangible
Inherent in the product	Created / sustained by communications
Copyable by competition	More difficult to copy
Changes as the technology develops/ needs to change	Sustainable over time
'Added value' primarily from company technological skills	'Added value' from company commitment to understanding and satisfying customers

Figure 12: Emotional and Functional Aspects of Branding

As can be deduced from the above table, brands will be more successful if they focus more on the emotional aspects. This is because competitors can copy the functional aspects of the brand and hence render any basis for competitive advantage obsolete. However, it can be stated that no two brands are perceived in the same manner when it comes to the level of consumers' emotional attachments.

Brand Facets

In essence, a brand is essentially a seller's promise to deliver a specific set of features, benefits and services consistently to the buyers. In fact, a brand can convey up to six levels of meanings (Aaker, 2004):

1) **Attributes**. A brand brings to mind certain attributes. Mercedes suggests expensive, well-built, well-engineered, durable and prestige automobiles.

2) **Benefits**. Attributes must be translated into functional and emotional benefits. The attribute 'expensive' translates into the emotional benefit that 'the car makes me feel important and admired'.

3) **Values**. The brand also says something about the producer's values. Mercedes stands for high performance, safety and prestige.

4) **Culture**. The brand may represent a certain culture. Mercedes represents German culture: organized, efficient and high quality.

5) **Personality**. The brand can project a certain personality.

6) **User**. The potential user might be someone with a relatively high income, such as a company CEO.

Benefits of Branding to Consumers

- Predictability and consistency – knowing what to expect every time consumers buy the brand
- Accountability – in situations where the brand does not deliver on its promise, consumers can feel they can hold the brand accountable such as asking for refunds or instigating legal actions.
- Easy identification, which make shopping easier – Nike is well known for its Swoosh sign and this makes it easier for consumers to identify its products and save time searching for the products, especially when shopping in stores.
- Quality of the product – every time a brand name is mentioned, we immediately form associations with it, especially in terms of its quality. For example, Virgin Atlantic is renowned for its excellence in customer services.
- Emotional rewards – brands satisfy more than the physical benefits (what the brand does). In fact, for some brands, the emotional satisfaction or benefits (how the brand make people feel) is what actually drives consumers to it.
- Risk reduction, reassurance and trust – these are an extension of the emotional connotations that brands convey. Rolex is expensive compared to other watches, but it conveys high feelings of trust, reliability and performance.

Benefits of Branding to Firms

- Means of identification to simplify tracing – this makes it much easier for consumers of the brand to identify the brand.
- Means of legally protecting unique features – this makes it legally difficult or impossible for other firms to copy the brand's name or other proprietary assets.
- Signal of quality level to satisfied customers – consumers can determine the quality of the brand and this makes it easier and enhances their purchasing decisions.
- Means of endowing products with unique associations – brands have associations. For example, Nike is associated with innovation, excellence and active lifestyles.
- Source of competitive advantage – the unique associations of the brand provides a basis for differentiating it from competing brands.
- Source of financial returns – the most popular brands are often the most profitable. This is because consumers appreciate its unique physical and emotional benefits and so are willing to buy and patronize the brands over long periods.
- Attract shelf space – this implies that the popularity of the brand will compel retailers to stock and sell it mainly because consumers will ask for it.
- Creates customer loyalty – people are definitely loyal to brands based on the brand's abilities to satisfy consumer's needs. This satisfaction is the basis for long-term consumer loyalty because consumers do not normally bother to search for competition brands if the brand is able to meet their requirements.

Steps in Building a Brand

Building a brand is very important and generally involves a sequence of steps, with each one contingent on achieving the previous step.

1) **Establish Brand Identity.** Identify the brand with customers and associate the brand in customer's minds with a specific product class or customer need

2) **Establish Brand Meaning.** Establish the totality of brand meaning in the minds of customers by linking a host of tangible and intangible brand associations with certain properties

3) **Determine Brand Responses.** Elicit the proper customer responses to this brand identification and meaning

4) **Establish Brand Relationships.** Convert brand responses to create an intense, active loyalty relationship between customers and the brand

Important Factors in Brand Building

Building a successful brand implies developing a product that has a unique and sustainable competitive advantage. It involves the following:

Figure 13: Aspects of Brand Building

- **Good quality product** – this implies that the brand must deliver on its promise, particularly in regard to the core benefits that it promises and which consumers expect. Quality therefore means conformity with the brand's promise and performance.
- **First mover advantage** – successful brands are always forward thinking and tend to be industry leaders as opposed to followers. This implies

that such brands set the standard in their respective industries by being the first to innovate and subsequently capture huge market share and are top in terms of consumer brand recall. Brands such as Coca-Cola, Apple iPhone and Google define their respective standards.

- **Distinct positioning / Repositioning** – this implies that the brand must occupy a clear, unique and often superior position in consumer's minds. Such positioning can be achieved by adopting strategies based on product associations, image, features, benefits, users, cultural symbols and the competition. In some cases, especially when the brand has experienced major crisis, there will be the need to reposition. The objective of such repositioning is to change consumers' perceptions towards the brand without which they may defect to a competing brand.

- **Strong communication programme** – successful brand development is contingent upon a strong communications programme in order to ensure that messages shaping consumers' perceptions of the brands are effective and well communicated. Such perceptions formed via communications programmes will shape consumers' beliefs and attitudes and ultimately their motivations to buy and consume the brand.

- **Time and consistency** – building a successful brand takes time, and firms must invest for the long term and not necessarily for short-term profits. Therefore, patience is key. Equally important is the need to invest significant resources in creating high levels of awareness, quality and ultimately customer loyalty. Today, some of the most successful brands include those that have been around for many years – Louis Vuitton was founded in 1854, Harvard University was founded in 1636 and MacDonald's in 1955.

- **Internal Marketing** – this implies that the employees of the company must completely buy into the brand and its values so that they can relate these in their daily operations and service interactions with external consumers. The employees are the company's first customers and they must subscribe to the values of the brand.

Brand Identity

Brand identity represents how the brand wants to be perceived by consumers and other stakeholders and is the starting point for building brands. Therefore, the firm must take deliberate efforts in forming, shaping and driving the brand identity in the minds of consumers. This is extremely important because ultimately firms should own and determine how consumers perceive the brand. It should not be a matter of consumers forming their independent judgements. Instead the firm should be able to influence its consumers into forming the desired brand perceptions. This is why it is agreed that brand identity emanates from the brand owner. The company's own communications are the single most important manner of relaying and forming brand identity in the minds of its consumers. In addition, such communications must emphasize the aspects of the brand that the firm wants consumers to remember, such as values, heritage, quality, price and prestige.

Brand image, on the other hand, relates to how consumers actually perceive the brand and is situated on the side of consumers. Such images can be formed because of any of the following:

- Company's own brand communications (advertisements)
- Consumer's previous experiences with the brand
- Recommendations or opinions of friends and family

It is very important that the brand identity (how the brand wants to be perceived) resonates with the brand image (how consumers actually perceive the brand), otherwise a brand mismatch happens, which is dangerous for the survival and success of the brand.

Steps in Creating Brand Identity

To have a clear and objective self-image of the brand identity is necessary in order for a brand to influence the desired set of brand awareness, perceived value and brand image.

Brand identity declares its **background,** its **principles,** its **purpose** and its **ambitions.** For that reason, brands need to be managed for consistency and vitality. Hence the identity concept, the promise to a customer, plays a crucial role within the brand management process. The brand must deliver coherent signs and products and it needs to be realistic. Brand image can easily change over time where brand identity represents long-lasting values of the brand. From that perspective, brand image is more a tactical asset, whereas brand identity fulfils a strategic asset role.

Aaker's Brand Identity Model

David Aaker is one of the most acclaimed writers and brand visionaries. He currently serves as the Vice Chairman of the Brand Consultancy firm Prophet as well as a visiting professor at the University of California, Berkeley Haas. Aaker developed his brand identity model around four different perspectives and twelve dimensions.

Brand managers should have an in-depth understanding of the brand identity from different perspectives before they are able to clarify, enrich and differentiate the brand identity.

1) Brand as a product
2) Brand as an organization
3) Brand as a person
4) Brand as a symbol

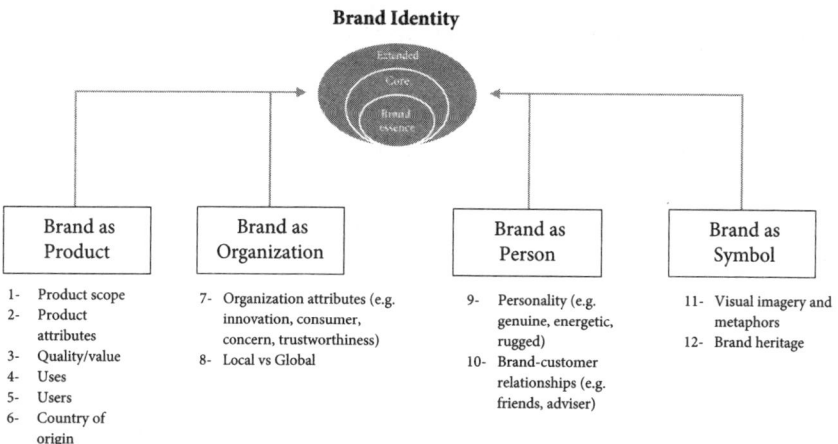

Figure 14: Aaker's Brand Identity Framework

1. Brand as a product

The product-related attributes will by nature have an important influence on brand identity because they are linked to user requirements and product experience.

Aaker addressed six dimensions within this group namely:

1) **Product scope** – the number of products that can be found in the organization's portfolio
2) **Product attributes** – the characteristics that are attributed to the brand
3) **Product quality** – the abilities of the product to meet the expectations of its consumers
4) **Product user** – the intended target audience for the product
5) **Product uses** – the supporting reasons why consumers should buy the product
6) **Product country of origin** – where the product originates

2. Brand as an organization

By looking at the brand as an organization, brand managers are forced to shift their perspective from product to organization attributes. These are less tangible and more subjective. Attributes as CRM, innovation, perceived quality, visibility and presence can contribute significantly towards value propositions and customer relationships.

Aaker addressed two dimensions within this group, namely:

1) **Organizational attributes** – innovation, trustworthiness, customer friendliness
2) **Local or global** – whether the brand is local, national, international or global

3. Brand as a Person

Brand as a person takes the perspective that the brand is a human being. Brand personality is a very distinctive brand element and extensively used in many brand equity models.

Aaker addressed two dimensions within this group namely:

1) **Personality:** for example, genuine, energetic, funny
2) **Brand/customer relationship**: consumers' perceptions of the brand as being, for example, caring or friendly

4. Brand as a Symbol

Brand as a symbol can capture almost anything that represents the brand. A strong symbol can fulfil an important and even a dominant role in brand strategy. Symbols are very strong if they involve a recognizable, meaningful and trustful metaphor.

Aaker addressed two dimension groups:

1) **Visual imagery and metaphor** – logos or slogans
2) **Brand heritage** – its origins and history

Choosing Brand Name Elements

Choosing brand names is arguably one of the most critical aspects of building and developing a brand. The brand name is one of the main aspects of brand identity, along with slogans, jingles and logos.

Six major considerations should be taken into consideration when choosing brand names.

1) **Memorable** – easy to remember. Many companies today are choosing fruits as brand names because these are often very easy to remember.
2) **Meaningful** – conveying information about the function of the product (e.g. Virgin Trains).
3) **Likeable** – visually, verbally and aesthetically appealing to consumers
4) **Transferable** – implies that the name should be capable of allowing the brand to be extended or diversified in different industries. For example, the name Virgin is flexible and can be diversified whereas

a brand such as Toys R Us would not be considered very transferable because the name itself is limiting.

5) **Adaptable** – ability of the brand to remain relevant and keep up with changing times. This may involve adopting a new logo, slogan or colours.

6) **Protectable** – this implies the ability of the brand to garner sustainable copyrights, trademarks and patent protection rights.

Brand Architecture/Hierarchy/Name Strategies

Organizations can draw from any of the following strategies, or even a combination:

1) **House of Brands Strategy** – this strategy involves distinct brands that are created for specific segments of the market and not associated with the corporate brand. Companies such as Unilever, Harley Davidson and Proctor and Gamble adopt this strategy.

2) **Branded House Strategy** – this involves using a single corporate brand across all the products and entities in the portfolio. Virgin and Armani adopt this approach.

3) **Hybrid Strategy** – this involves a combination of the two strategies mentioned above. Marriott is a proponent of this strategy.

Brand Positioning

Positioning relates to how the firm's brands are perceived by consumers. In other words, what comes to consumers' minds when the firm's products and services are mentioned? Firms can position their brands in consumers based on any of the following positioning strategies:

- **Product use or application** – Advil for pain relief
- **Product user** – Coutts Bank in the UK is known to target high net worth individuals for its banking services

- **Price and quality** – Ryanair is known for affordable air travel but never emphasizes the quality of services
- **Product feature** – Apple IPhone come with Siri feature
- **Product class** – Whole Foods is known for its organic product range
- **Competition** – Boots v Superdrug in the UK. Boots mentions in its advertisements that 'the only thing that is not super about Superdrug are its prices'
- **Benefit** – provided to its consumers. Volvo for safety
- **Country of origin** – German car manufacturers such as Mercedes capitalize on the country's strong reputation for engineering

Positioning/Perceptual Map

Perceptual (or positioning) mapping is a marketing tool that enables marketers to plot the position of their offering against those of the competition.

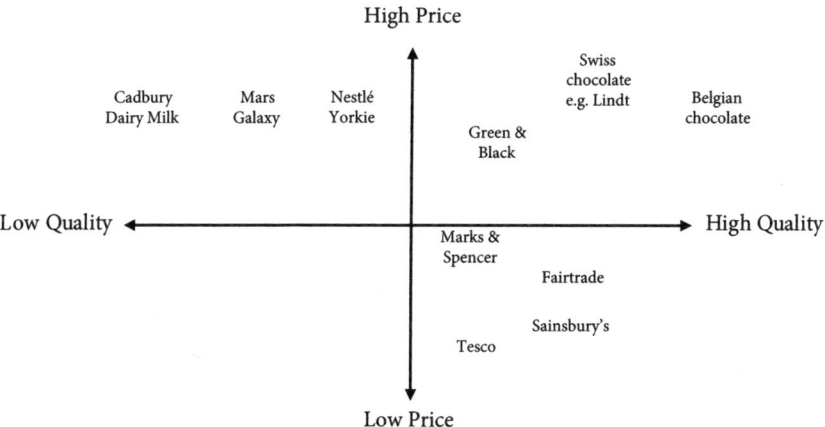

Figure 15: Example positioning map of the UK chocolate block sector market

Questions

1) Choose a brand. Then attempt to identify its sources of brand equity. Assess its levels of brand awareness and the strength, favourability and uniqueness of its associations.

2) Choose two of your favourite brands. Which brand elements do you immediately associate with these brands? In your opinion, how do these brands fulfil the criteria for good brand elements?

3) Choose a brand. Identify and explain its brand portfolio and brand architecture. Propose recommendations for improving the chosen company's branding strategies.

4) The Virgin brand has been extended into many different industries such as airlines, trains, gyms, media and soon space tourism. Evaluate Virgin's branding strategy.

CHAPTER TEN

The Price Mix

Once the organization has produced its product, it must then work on its pricing. Price is defined as the measure of value offered in exchange between sellers and buyers and is critically important to the success of a product. The measure of value denotes the benefits that customers will derive from buying and consuming the product, and the higher the value placed on the product, the more willing will be customers to pay the price. Having the best product should be complemented by setting the right price if the product is to succeed in the market. In the final analysis, the price charged can directly influence the firm's market share and, ultimately, its profitability. This is because even a small change in price can help in generating higher profits.

The importance of price is underlined by the following reasons:

- Price is the only element or aspect of the marketing mix that generates revenue for the firm. This is because all the other elements – product, place, promotion, people, process and physical evidence – cost money.
- Price serves as a basis for competitive differentiation. This implies that firms can use price as a means of showing that the products sold are superior or more competitive and vice versa.
- Price is also a signal of the quality of the product offered which implies that price determines quality. Generally speaking, the higher the price, the higher the quality as perceived by consumers.
- Unlike the other elements of the marketing mix, such as product and distribution, pricing is flexible and can be changed and adjusted at short notice to reflect the changing market dynamics.

Factors Affecting Pricing Decisions

Pricing is without doubt one of the most difficult decisions for managers to make. This is because there are so many factors and issues to take into consideration before deciding and determining the final price for products. The following factors should be considered:

- **Cost of production** – This is the starting point for determining the price of the product. In most cases and logically speaking, the price set should not be lower than the actual cost of producing the product.
- **Demand** – This refers to the quantities that consumers are willing and prepared to buy. Generally speaking, the higher the demand, the higher the price tends to be – and vice versa. This factor is particularly critical to firms that produce seasonal goods.
- **Competition** – Competition can be difficult to avoid and is a fact of modern-day business, especially considering that very few true monopolies operate nowadays. Therefore, this implies that managers tasked with making pricing decisions must conduct competitor research before setting their final prices for products.
- **Availability of substitutes** – These are products that can more or less satisfy similar customer needs, such as coffee and tea. The availability or otherwise of substitute products can affect the prices charged for products in the sense that where there are no substitutes available, then the firm can charge higher prices and vice versa.
- **Company or organizational objectives** – Every organization will have predetermined objectives, such as increasing profitability. Pricing can therefore be critical in contributing towards the attainment of such objectives. It could be the case of reducing product prices to generate more sales and ultimately profits.
- **Taxation** – Companies pay taxes to governments, which can include corporate taxes as well as value added tax. Typically, whenever governments increase taxes, most firms will respond by charging higher prices for their products.

- **Interest rates** – Many firms borrow to invest in growing their businesses. Such borrowing is tied to interest payments on the loans secured. This can have an impact upon the prices charged by the firm.
- **Inflation levels** – Inflation is the general rise in price levels, and such prices could be related to the aspects associated with the production and provision of products sold by firms. For example, increases in the cost of petrol, which affects transportation of goods, can eventually affect the firm's pricing decisions.
- **Quality perceptions** – Quality is subjective and means different things to different people. However, such relative perceptions of the products produced by the firm can affect the prices that customers are willing to pay for its products.
- **Stage of product in the PLC** – The product life cycle explains the different stages that products go through in their lifespans. Different firms adopt different pricing decisions depending on the stage of the product in its life cycle. For example, in some cases, lower prices are set at the introduction and decline stages but then increased in the growth stage.
- **Income levels** – The levels of disposable income vary depending on factors such as geographical location. This explains why in some cases, the same product will have different prices. More specifically, areas with high income residents will tend to attract higher prices as compared to locations populated by people with less disposable incomes.

Price Setting Methods

There are a number of methods or approaches that organizations can adopt and apply when setting the prices for their products:

1) Value-based pricing
2) Cost-based pricing
3) Competition-based pricing
4) Demand-based pricing

Value-Based Pricing

This approach is based on first assessing and determining customers' needs and perceptions of value and then setting the price afterwards. These assessments of consumer perceptions of value are factored into the design and production of the product. Therefore, this approach is unique in the sense that pricing decisions are made in reverse order: the needs of customers and their value expectations are identified first, and the product is then produced to meet such value expectations. Such perceptions of value can include all the aspects of the marketing mix, such as services. The emphasis is on the company to convince customers via its marketing communications efforts of the extra value added, which then attracts them to buy its products.

Cost-Based Pricing

As the name implies, cost-based pricing implies that the firm will set its prices based on the relative costs associated with producing the products plus a margin of profit on top of such costs. These costs include production, transportation, distribution and selling of the product. This approach is one of the most popular approaches adopted by companies because these costs can be calculated and determined more easily than value-based pricing.

Typically, there are two types of such costs – namely, fixed and variable costs. Fixed costs are sometimes called overheads and will always be incurred. These do not necessarily change regardless of production or sales generated. Examples of such fixed costs include rent, employee salaries and utilities.

Variable costs, on the other hand, change with the levels of production. For every unit of the product produced, the costs involved will vary and go up depending on the actual number of units produced.

The sum of the fixed costs and the variable costs for any given level of production is known as Total Costs. It is critical that the firm manages its costs well to be able to generate profits at the same time as it remains competitive.

The most commonly used cost-based pricing approach is the **cost-plus pricing** approach. This implies that the firm will first determine the cost of producing the product and then add a mark-up as its profit. This approach is simple, though it tends to ignore consumer demand and can actually affects firm's competitiveness.

Competition-Based Pricing

This approach is driven by competitors' actions and implies matching the prices set by the firm's competitors. The firm will need to carefully study and understand its competitors' actions – such as strategies, costs, prices, products and services – and then use such information to set its own prices. This approach shows the firm's ambitions and intentions to compete strongly. However, this approach might involve the firms trying to match a much bigger and stronger competitor, which can lead to its demise very quickly.

Demand-Based Pricing

This approach implies that prices are set based on the quantities that consumers are willing and prepared to pay. In other words, the prices charged fluctuate with demand levels. Therefore, when demand is high, the firm charges higher prices and vice versa. Firms that sell seasonal products such as ice cream, air travel and hotels typically adopt this approach.

PRICING STRATEGIES

Pricing strategies help explain how firms can use pricing in order to achieve their set objectives. In other words, firms can manipulate the prices of their products to boost sales by means of adopting these pricing strategies.

Pricing Strategies for New Products

There are three pricing strategies which can be adopted by firms when developing price strategies for their new products:

- Market penetration pricing
- Market skimming
- Early cash recovery strategies

Market Penetration Pricing Strategy

Market penetration strategy/objective: This implies setting an initial low price to stimulate demand and increase market share and then raising the price afterwards. Due to the high volume of sales, it is expected that costs will fall, and this allows the firms to offer even lower prices for its products. Market penetration strategy is appropriate under three conditions:

- The market is price sensitive, and relatively low prices will attract additional sales
- Low prices will discourage new competitors
- Unit costs will fall with increased output (economies of scale)

Market Skimming Pricing Strategy

Market skimming strategy/objective: This involves setting a high initial price for a new product in order to take advantage of those buyers who are ready to pay a much higher price and then reducing the price afterwards.

This strategy is appropriate under three conditions:

- There is insufficient production capacity and competitors cannot increase capacity
- Some buyers are relatively insensitive to high prices
- High price is perceived as high quality

Early Cash Recovery Pricing Strategy

The strategy or objective is to recover high investment costs by charging high prices in the short to medium term. It is mostly adopted by drug manufacturing companies such as GlaxoSmithKline, which incur high capital investments in terms of research and need to recoup these investment costs and make profits before the patent for such products expire.

This strategy is appropriate under three conditions:

- The business is high risk
- Rapid changes in fashion or technology are expected
- The innovator is short of cash

Pricing Strategies for Existing Products

For products that are already in the market, firms can also employ a number of pricing strategies to help in generating more demand and ultimately sales:

- Psychological pricing strategy
- Product Bundle pricing strategy
- Promotional pricing strategy
- Price Discrimination or Segmented pricing strategy

Psychological Pricing Strategy

This strategy implies charging pricing based on such considerations as consumers' perceptions of quality, reference points that consumers carry in their minds in terms of what constitutes a fair price, and the use of even and odd numbers in prices. Most consumers do not invest time or effort or have the skills in determining whether they are paying a fair price for products. They rely on their intuition when assessing product prices, as well as cues. However, most of these cues emanate from the selling firm and can include price guarantees, aftersales services, free delivery or extended warranties.

The use of even and odd numbers are widely used, especially in the UK, where even very high-end expensive brands will use odd numbers in their pricing. For example, the use of £9.99 and not £10.00 is very prevalent in the UK. Firms use this strategy to make consumers believe that the product is less than £10, even though the difference is just one penny!

Promotional Pricing

This strategy implies that firms will offer massive price discounts on products with the aim of generating excitement and urgency and ultimately increased consumer purchases. In some cases, firms will even offer the product below cost of producing the product. This strategy is widely used in Europe and the United States, where firms tie such discounts to special events like Boxing Day sales in the UK (26 December) or the Independence Day sale (4 July) in the United States. This strategy is used for a limited time only: firms cannot afford to continue this practice for an extended time due to its impact on their bottom lines. Another reason for adopting this strategy is that it allows firms to clear out any excess or post-season stock they may have.

Product Bundle Pricing

This strategy is typically adopted by firms that sell a multitude of products, which tend to be complementary. This means that such products are often consumed together – hence the term 'bundle'. Therefore, the prices for all such products are combined into one reduced price, which is lower than if the products were bought as single items. For example, XFinity in the United States and Virgin in the UK both offer phone, television and Internet services at a reduced bundle price. Burger King also uses a 'combo' price for meal deals that include burger, fries and drinks.

Price Discrimination of Segmented Pricing

This strategy implies that the firm will sell the same product at different prices based on such considerations as location and consumer profiles.

In terms of location, the firm may charge a different price because the cost of operations, such as rent, are higher. In terms of customer profile, the firm may charge different prices because of the income level of people. A classic example of this strategy is that firms operating out of Oxford Street, which is England's busiest business thoroughfare, will charge higher prices for products because this location is mostly frequented by tourists, who generally do not mind paying higher prices. However, the same firm will sell the same product in Kent for at least 20 per cent less.

CHAPTER ELEVEN

The Place Mix

The place mix is the third element of the marketing mix and refers to the channels of distribution that firms can use in order to ensure that consumers have ready and easy access to their products. The place mix is all about making the firm's products available to its consumers in the right place. Modern-day consumers expect firms to make their products available to them where and when they want it. Otherwise, consumers will switch their loyalties to competitors that can match their ever-changing expectations. Therefore, it is imperative that firms do the research to identify the most optimal distribution channels that allow the products to reach consumers in the right place, at the right time and in the right quantities.

The channels of distribution consist of intermediaries or middlemen who serve as links between the manufacturer and the final users of the product. These intermediaries can include supermarkets or websites, such as Amazon.

Functions or Roles of Intermediaries

Intermediaries play a critical function in ensuring that manufacturer's products reach consumers at the right time, at the right place and in the right quantities. In summary, their functions include the following.

- They gather information about potential and current customers
- They develop and disseminate persuasive communications to stimulate purchasing
- They reach agreement on price so that transfer of ownership can be effected

- They acquire funds to finance inventories
- They place orders with manufacturers
- They assume risks connected with carrying out channel work
- They provide storage space and transport of goods

Distribution Channels

There are a number of distribution channels that firms can use in ensuring that their products reach customers. Wholesalers typically buy and sell in bulk or large quantities from manufacturers to consumers. Retailers tend to buy in bulk from manufacturers and then sell to consumers in units or small quantities.

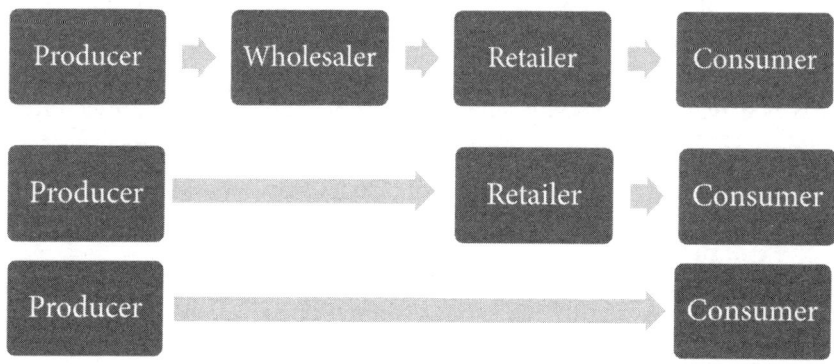

Figure 16: Channels of Distribution

These channels are:

- Direct distribution
- Indirect distribution
- Hybrid distribution

Direct Distribution Channels

As the name implies, this practice involves the firm making its product available to consumers through its own channels. These channels can be via its own stores or its website. It can be more expensive for firms using this strategy but has the advantage of maintaining control and reliability.

Indirect Distribution Channels

This practice implies that the manufacturer uses the services of intermediaries to make its products available to consumers. Therefore, the firm does not involve the actual distribution of its products but rather employs the services on retailers and wholesalers in the distribution of its products. The advantage of this approach is that it is relatively cheaper for the manufacturer, who does not have to carry the costs associated with operating a retail outlet such as rent, insurance, utilities and hiring of distribution personnel.

Hybrid Distribution Channels

This is a relatively evolving channel, which involves the manufacturer using a combination of direct and indirect distribution approaches or practices. The firm will operate its own distribution outlets as well as using the services of retailers and wholesalers. Many hotels and airlines now adopt this strategy and it has the added advantage of reaching as many consumers as possible. In the case of airlines such as British Airways, it sells tickets both on its own website as well as using online ticketing websites such as Skyscanner for example. The same applies to hotels which sell hotels accommodation or rooms on their own websites and also using the distribution channel provided by such online accommodation retailers such as Hotels.com and Booking.com, for example.

Distribution Strategies

Distribution strategies identify and explain how firms can optimize the channels of distribution to reach the right consumer audiences and grow its sales. These strategies include the following.

- Intensive distribution strategy

- Selective distribution strategy
- Exclusive distribution strategy

Intensive Distribution Strategy

Intensive distribution implies that the firm will make its products as widely available in the market as possible in order to reach as many consumers as possible. This is the predominant strategy of firms that sell fast-moving consumer goods (FMCGs), which are products that are bought and consumed very regularly, such as water, cigarettes and milk. Consumers expect to be able to find such products widely available in the market in many convenient locations.

Selective Distribution Strategy

As the name implies, this strategy involves the firm making its product available to consumers to buy at some or few outlets, meaning that it is not widely available. Firms that tend to practise this strategy manufacture products that consumers buy on an irregular basis. Nike practises this strategy by making its products available only in its own outlets or in specific retail outlets.

Exclusive Distribution Strategy

This is the extreme form of distribution, whereby the firm makes a conscious decision to make its products available in only its own dedicated stores or using very few retailers. This strategy is typically practised by luxury brands such as Hermes and LVMH.

Factors to Consider when Choosing Distribution Channels

Choosing the right distribution channel is critical for the success of a firm's products. It is essential that the firm carefully assesses each of the following factors before making the final determination about the most optimal channel or channels to use in the distribution of its products.

The 7Cs, outlined below, provide a very useful basis for identifying and understanding the critical issues to take into consideration:

- **Characteristics of the product**
  The nature of the product made and offered by the firm can influence the relative choice of distribution channels. Such characteristics include a consideration of whether the product is durable or perishable. For example, perishable products such as roses will typically need a shorter channel of distribution because the product can easily wilt if it has to go through many channels before reaching the final consumer.

- **Consumer characteristics**
  The profile and attributes of the final consumer can also influence the choices of channel to be used in making the product available in the market. For example, millennials and Gen Z consumers prefer buying products online rather than visiting physical stores. Therefore, if these are the target audience, it is imperative that the firm makes its products available for purchase online.

- **Cost involved in distributing the product**
  The cost involved in using the different channels can ultimately affect the final price that end user consumers have to pay. The more channel members that are involved in distributing the product, the higher the price that end user consumers will have to pay. This is because each channel member will incur costs, from transportation, rent, storage and personnel. This helps to explain why buying online is relatively cheaper than buying in physical stores.

- **Control over channel members**
  Maintaining control of the product is critical to firms because retailers or other intermediaries might be engaged in practices that can ultimately harm the firm's brand. For example, retailers can add significantly high margins and charge higher prices, which can discourage end-user consumers from buying the product. In some cases, manufacturers will even allow retailers to return unsold products. The firm can therefore maintain more control of its products if it sells via its own channels

rather than using retailers who might be more interested in higher profit margins.

- **Competitor's choice of channel**

  The choices of channels used by the firm's competitors should also be taken into consideration when deciding on distribution channels. Most competitors tend to employ similar channels of distribution. For example, Coca-Cola and Pepsi both use retailers and wholesalers in the distribution of the products.

- **Channel availability in the marketplace**

  This consideration implies whether the firm's preferred choices of distribution are available in the market in which it operates. For example, selling online may not be possible in all locations in which the firm operates, so the firm may need to resort to traditional on the street retailers.

- **Characteristics of intermediaries**

  Intermediaries can provide additional value or benefit to the firm in terms of product distribution. This value can manifest in such ways as the intermediary's size and number of outlets, the countries in which the intermediary operates in and the perceived brand image of the intermediary. The firm can therefore benefit by leveraging on the additional benefits that the intermediary provides. For example, Walmart is the largest retailer in the world and firms that use Walmart for the distribution of their products will benefit from Walmart's huge geographical presence as well as the number of retail outlets it operates.

CHAPTER TWELVE

The Promotion Mix

The fourth element of the marketing mix is Promotion. Once the firm has produced its products, set its prices and determined channels of distribution, it should now focus on creating persuasive communications to its target audiences in order to create awareness and subsequent demand for its products. Without this awareness, consumers will not know of the existence of the firm's products and hence will not buy. Promotions or marketing communications refers to the exchange of marketing information between an organization and its publics. Publics include the following:

- Customers
- Shareholders
- Employees
- The government
- The local community in which the organization operates
- Trade unions
- Pressure groups
- The media

The Communication Process

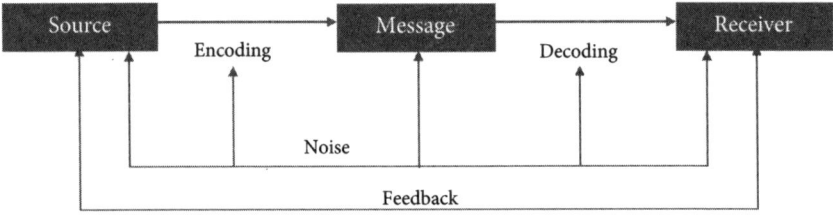

Figure 17: Linear Model of Communication

The elements of the communication model can be classified as follows:

- **Sender** – the party sending the message to another party
- **Encoding** – putting thought into symbolic form
- **Message** – the content of the communication that the sender sends to the receiver
- **Media** – the communication channels used for sending the message
- **Decoding** – the receiver translates and interprets message
- **Receiver** – the party receiving the message
- **Response** – the receiver reacting to the message
- **Feedback** – the part of the receiver's response which is communicated back to the sender
- **Noise** – factors that prevent the decoding of a message by the receiver in the way intended by the sender

Tasks Of Marketing Communications

The following points need to be considered:

- Who should receive the messages?
- What should the messages say?
- What image does the organization/brand want to project?
- How much money is to be spent?
- How to deliver the message?
- What action should the receivers take?
- How to control the whole process?
- Determining what was achieved by the firm's communication efforts.

Opinion Formers and Opinion Leaders

The effectiveness of marketing communications can be greatly impacted by opinion formers and leaders. The issues of trust and credibility are extremely important if the firm's marketing communications messages are to be well received by customers. If the brand name or communications are affiliated with unfavourable attitudes or are perceived negatively by the leaders and formers of the target group, this will have a varied negative affect on the perceptions and attitudes of target audiences.

With this in mind, it would be a smart idea to take these opinion leaders and formers into consideration when planning marketing strategies and campaigns. It is helpful to undertake research to find out just who the opinion formers of the target audience are; leaders are more difficult to identify because they will be different for different people, but it may be easier to find out which groups of people are often opinion leaders, perhaps family members, teachers, colleagues, etc. If communications take these people into consideration and aim to fulfil their needs as well, it may be possible to trigger a positive word of mouth, with a more positive effect on consumer purchase decision.

For this reason, firms can engage with opinion leaders and formers in crafting effective marketing communication messages.

Opinion Formers and Leaders

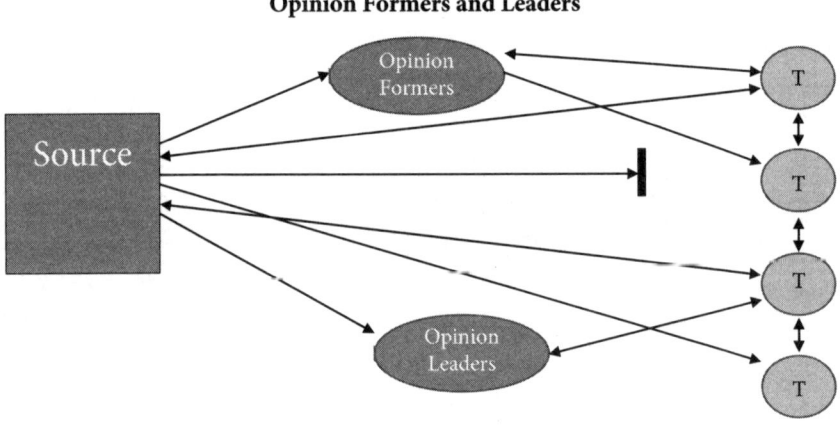

Figure 18: Opinion Formers and Leaders

- **Opinion leaders** are individuals predisposed to receiving information and then reprocessing it to influence other members of the group. They tend to belong to the same social class as the others but may enjoy higher social status. They have more influence than information received directly from the mass media and are more persuasive.

- **Opinion formers** are individuals able to exert personal influence on the others because of their authority, education or status associated with the object of the communication. For example, a pharmacist is consulted by consumers buying medicines.

Integrated Marketing Communications (IMC)

The concept under which a company carefully integrates and co-ordinates its many communication channels to deliver a clear, consistent and compelling message about the organization and its products. It is an approach to achieving the objectives of a marketing campaign, through a well-coordinated use of different promotional methods that are intended to reinforce each other.

As defined by the American Association of Advertising Agencies, an integrated marketing communications model 'recognizes the value of a comprehensive plan that evaluates the strategic roles of a variety of communication disciplines – advertising, public relations, personal selling and sales promotion – and combines them to provide clarity, consistency and maximum communication impact'.

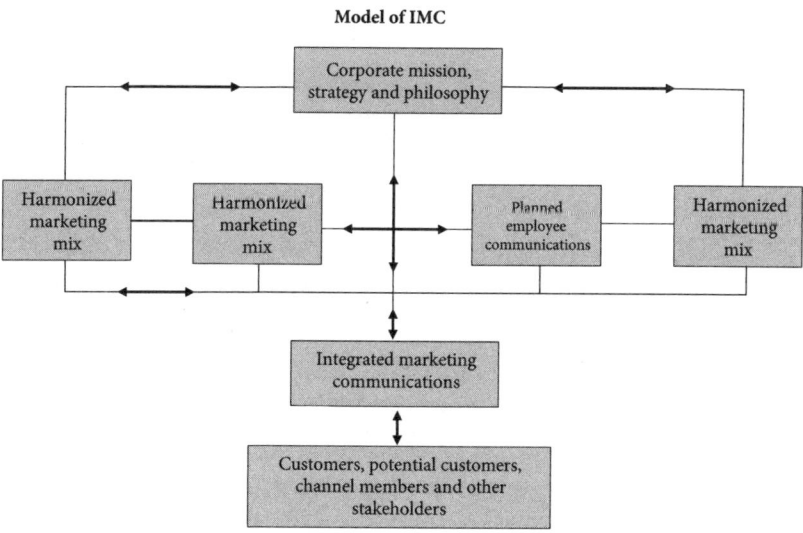

Model of IMC

Figure 19: Integrated Marketing Communications Model

Objectives of Promotions / Marketing Communications

Promotions are one of the most expensive aspects of marketing. However, its benefits cannot be overestimated and it is undertaken to achieve the following objectives. The DRIPE Framework best explains the purpose of marketing promotions:

D = Differentiate – the means of showing the uniqueness of the products promoted

R = Remind – aim at existing or previous customers to keep the product fresh in their minds and tempt them to buy again

I = Inform – aimed at prospective customers to convince them to buy the product

P = Persuade – convince both existing and prospective customers to buy the product

E = Engage – maintaining long-term relationships with customers

The Promotions Mix

The promotions mix refers to the tools, methods or techniques that marketers can use to promote the firm's products.

MARCOMS AND THE MARKETING MIX

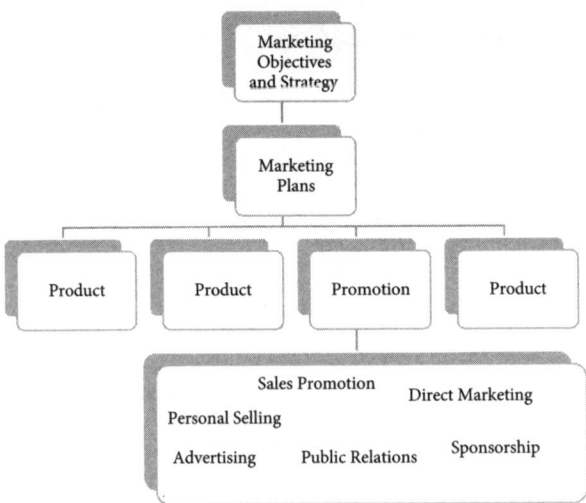

Figure 20: Marketing Communications and the Marketing Mix

The promotional mix consists of six techniques/tools/methods:

- Advertising
- Sales promotions
- Direct marketing
- Personal selling
- Public relations and
- Sponsorship

Advertising

Advertising can be defined as 'any paid-for form of non-personal communication effected through mass media by an identified sponsor' (Bovee, 1992). The AIDA framework explains the objectives of advertising:

A = Awareness
I = Interest
D = Desire
A = Action

Theories Of Advertising

There are two theories of advertising, namely strong and weak theories.

The strong theory is based on the premise that advertising can affect a degree of change in the knowledge, attitudes, beliefs or behaviours of target audiences. Exponents of this theory believe that advertising can persuade people to buy products that they have never previously purchased.

The weak theory stresses that a consumer's pattern of brand purchases is driven more by habit than exposure to promotional messages. This is based on Ehrenberg's (1997) ATR framework of Awareness, Trial and Reinforcement.

Advertising Frameworks

Many models and frameworks have been developed over the years to explain how advertising works:

The Sales framework is oriented mainly to direct response and is based on the premise that all advertising activities are aimed ultimately at shifting products – generating sales. Advertising is considered to have a short-term direct impact on sales, and it is on sales alone that the true effect of advertising is felt.

The Persuasion framework assumes that advertising works rationally because messages are capable of being persuasive. Persuasion is effected gradually, moving buyers through a number of sequential steps, and assumes that buyer decision-making is rational and can be accurately predicted.

The Involvement framework draws members of the target audience into the advertisement and elicits a largely emotional response. Involvement with the product develops because of involvement with the advertisement

The Salience framework is based upon the premise that advertising works by standing out, by being different from all other advertisements in the product class. It is also based on the assumption that the audience are active, rational problem solvers and are perfectly capable of discriminating among brands.

Advertising Media
- Broadcast media – includes television, radio and cinema
- Print media – includes newspapers, magazines and leaflets
- Outdoor media – includes billboards and posters
- Mobile media – relates to advertising on buses, taxis and trains
- New media – includes the use of social media, phones, SMS etc.

Above-the-line Media

A proportion of advertising expenditure is paid to an agency, for advertisements via:

- Commercial radio
- Commercial television
- The press – national, regional and local newspapers, and consumer, trade and technical magazines

Below-the-line Media

Paid for by agreed flat fee. No commission is involved.

- Public relations
- Sales promotion
- Direct marketing (including direct mail)
- Exhibitions
- Sales literature – leaflets, brochures, catalogues and manuals
- Point of sale material
- Sponsorship
- Promotional videos

Key Media Concepts

- Reach – the number of different people exposed to the message
- Frequency – degree of exposure repetition (i.e., the number of times each person sees the ad)
- Efficiency – cost per thousand (CPM). The cost of reaching 1,000 households or 1,000 target readers
- Reach and Frequency are combined to determine audience impact

Pros and Cons of Different Advertising Media

The different advertising media explained earlier have distinct advantages and shortcomings, which are outlined below.

Television

Advantages

- High impact, combining colour, sound and motion
- High reach achievable over a short time
- Cost efficient (CPM)
- Mass market with audience flexibility

Limitations

- Costs are high in terms of both absolute cost and production costs
- High waste and Empty Chair Syndrome implying that people switch channels during adverts
- Clutter in that a high level of repetition is necessary
- Increasing level of fragmentation
- Long lead times in that it takes a long time to produce and schedule television adverts

Newspapers

Advantages

- Wide reach
- High coverage
- Low costs
- Very flexible
- Short lead times
- Good communication of detailed messages
- Targetting of specific audiences
- Immediacy, offering short-term tactical opportunities
- Direct response from consumers is possible

Limitations

- Short lifespan
- Advertisements get little exposure
- Lower reach and frequency than television
- Variable reproduction
- Passive

Consumer magazines

Advantages

- Flexible targetting opportunities
- Image association
- High-quality environment/reproduction
- Long shelf life/pass on readerships (magazines shared with others)
- Strong media–reader relationships
- Specific and specialized target audience
- Low relative cost

Limitations

- Slower frequency build up
- Expensive to achieve high coverage
- Long lead times

Radio

Advantages

- Good for frequency
- Good targetting possible
- Short lead times allows tactical/promotional usage
- Excellent platform for creativity
- Low costs – absolute, relative and production
- Flexible – open to promotion tie-ins, etc.

Limitations

- Lacks impact – audio dimension only
- Difficult to get audience attention
- Low prestige

Outdoor media (Billboards)

Advantages

- High reach and frequency
- Low relative costs
- Good coverage as a support medium

- Location oriented
- National, regional and local coverage possible
- Increasing levels of site innovation
- Big, bold, dominant media. Allows for clear branding messages

Limitations
- Poor image (but improving)
- Long production time
- Difficult to measure
- Message limitation due to short exposure time

Overview of New and Social Media Paid Channels of Communications

In recent years, there has been an explosion in the growth and use of social media channels such as Facebook and Twitter for example. This growth is explained by the fact that such channels offer unparalleled access to consumers with similar characteristics based on demographic, geographic and psychographic attributes. There are also the added benefits of enabling the firm to build, maintain and develop a brand voice and presence; emphasizing on its marketing messages to consumers; monitoring and obtaining first-hand feedback from customers as well as engagement with customers.

Some of the most popular social media channels include Facebook, Twitter, Instagram, Pinterest and TikTok and these are reviewed as follows:

Facebook

Facebook is now described in some quarters as the largest continent in the world because of the huge volume of subscribers – some 2.7 billion active followers. Facebook makes most of its money from advertising: in the third quarter of 2020 alone, it made $22.22 from advertising revenues. Among users of the channel, 80 per cent access it via mobile devices (Sproutsocial, 2020).

- Users 65 years and older are the fastest-growing group on Facebook. In 2019, the most significant change in Facebook user demographics was among users born in 1945 or earlier, also known as the 'Silent' generation. This age group had grown on the platform from 26 per cent in 2018 to nearly 40 per cent in 2019. Interestingly, Millennials and Boomers only increased by a maximum of 2 per cent and Gen Xers even reduced their Facebook use.
- Fewer teens are using Facebook now than in previous years. In 2015, 71 per cent of teens were active on Facebook. Currently, only 51 per cent of American teenagers between 13 and 17 years old use Facebook. While it's still more than half of US teenagers, businesses need to keep this data in mind when creating targeting ads and content.
- Only 10 per cent of Facebook users live in the US or Canada. Even though Asian-Pacific users comprise nearly 41.3 per cent of monthly active users (MAU) on Facebook, US and Canada's 10.1 per cent MAUs shouldn't be dismissed so quickly. Just over 48 per cent of Facebook Ad revenue comes from the United States and Canada alone. Businesses with an international presence, or serve international audiences, have a tremendous opportunity to reach ad markets with lower competition than North American markets.
- 74 per cent of high-income earners are Facebook users. Facebook use is prominent among high-earners, and even surpasses LinkedIn, which reaches just 49 per cent of users making more than $75,000. YouTube is the only social media platform with more reach at 83 per cent of high-income earners.
- 1.62 billion users visit Facebook daily. While it might seem like there's an urge to use social media less, the data shows otherwise. Facebook's overall active users continue to increase every year across the platform as a whole. Among active US Facebook users, 74 per cent of people use the site every day.

- 88 per cent of Facebook users are on the platform to stay in contact with friends and family. Where people once had to make long-distance calls to keep in touch with friends and family, people are now only a click away from maintaining better relationships. According to Statista, Facebook is a platform all demographics use to stay in touch.

- Highest traffic occurs mid-day Wednesday and Thursday. The days and times advertisers post on social media can impact the engagement on your posts. Our report on the best times to post on every social media platform found that between 11 a.m. and 2 p.m. on Wednesday and Thursday are the best time to post on Facebook to reach the most people. Of course, depending on the firm's audience and industry, the highest engagement times might differ slightly. Testing when the firm's audience is most engaged can help firms create a social media content calendar that shares posts at the optimal times on each platform.

- Facebook Stories has 300 million active users daily. While Instagram Stories is slightly more popular, Facebook Stories proves to grow as a place where Facebook users spend a lot of time. Creating Facebook Stories requires a different marketing strategy than creating other types of Facebook posts. If the firm's audience is active on Stories, it's worth it to invest in creating content tailored to that medium.

- 94 per cent of Facebook Ad revenue is from mobile. A mere 6 per cent of Facebook's advertising revenue comes from desktop-only users. People continue to access Facebook primarily from mobile, which drives advertisers to spend more money targeting mobile users. This information also serves as a reminder of how important it is to optimize all of the firm's social media content to be as mobile-friendly as possible (Sproutsocial, 2020).

Among the benefits of advertising on Facebook can be mentioned the following:

- Huge reach – Facebook divides its reach into organic, paid and viral. Organic reach is the number of people who have seen a post in the news feed, in the ticker and on the page itself. Paid reach is the number of unique people who have seen an advertisement or a sponsored story. Viral reach is the number of unique people who have seen a story about a page published by a friend. This huge reach potential enables forms and brands to instantly generate brand awareness among a community of people spread all over the world. It also provides added benefits and features that makes it possible for firms and advertisers to target very specific segments of users based on such characteristics or attributes as age, gender, political orientation, interests and so on. This targeting capability makes it possible for advertisers to reach their target audiences more efficiently and effectively.

- However, there are also downsides to using Facebook. These include the fact that users can choose which posts to follow, which thus limits the whole target audience intended. Another downside is the risk of a 'firestorm', which implies that users can target a company's social network presence to post negative comments, particularly when a company is facing a crisis. There is also the issue of managing users' data in terms of privacy and sharing permission, which can create legal, ethical and reputational challenges.

- Followers – The number of Facebook followers provides a good but basic metric for capturing the reach and popularity of a given message.

- Likes and shares – The number of likes provides a good indication as regards the levels of customer engagement with the advertiser's messages. Also, the number of shares does indicate the extent to how viral the advertiser's message is.

Twitter

Twitter is the second largest social media channel besides Facebook. It has some 340 million users, some 500 million tweets are sent daily, and generated advertising revenues of $1.6 billion in 2020. Twitter Demographics includes the following (Omnicore Agency, 2020)

- 24 per cent of all US Twitter users are male, whereas 21 per cent of US Twitter users are female.

- 22 per cent of US adults use Twitter.
- 24 per cent of all Internet male users use Twitter, whereas 21 per cent of all Internet Female users use Twitter.
- There are 262 million International Twitter users (users outside the US).
- Roughly 42 per cent of Twitter users are on the platform daily.
- The US accounts for just 36 million monetizable daily active Twitter users.
- 32 per cent of US Twitter users have higher college degrees.
- The total number of Twitter users in the UK is 15.25 million.
- 38 per cent of US Twitter users are between the ages of 18 and 29, 26 per cent of users are 30–49 years old.
- 77 per cent of Americans who earn $75,000 or more use Twitter.
- 80 per cent of Twitter users are affluent millennials.
- 93 per cent of Twitter community members are open to brands getting involved, if done so in the right way.
- The top three countries by user count outside the US are Japan (49.1 million users), India (17 million) and Brazil (15.7 million).
- 80 per cent of Twitter users accessing the platform on a mobile device, and 93 per cent of video views are on mobile.

Twitter provides many benefits to firms advertising their products on its channel. Firstly, every tweet or Twitter message goes directly to followers and such tweets are easy to create. This makes it possible for advertising firms to communicate directly to its followers. This can be particularly beneficial in resolving customer service challenges or issues. Firms can create a Twitter Handle to improve engagement and interactions with customers especially in resolving customer complaints and providing prompt response to such complaints.

However, Twitter advertising suffers from 'tweet overflow', making it very difficult for the firm's messages to stand out and gain customer attention. Also, because tweets are limited to 280 characters, it makes it harder to include visual content.

Instagram

Instagram turned ten years old in 2020 and it's safe to say that the social networking app has changed many lives during its existence. The visual-centric platform that began as a photo-posting app has grown into a source of income for creators and a new sales channel for businesses. Compared to Facebook, Instagram is a network of younger users. It's projected that the number of Instagram users in the US will reach 125.5 million active users by 2023. The network surpassed the 1 billion monthly active user mark in June 2018. According to Statista (2020), more than half of the global Instagram user population is younger than 34 years old. It's the second most preferred app after Snapchat for teenagers in the US.

Instagram has been able to maintain its user base fairly consistently over the last year. In 2019, the percentage of US adults who use Instagram rose from 35 per cent to 37 per cent and the active reported users have held steady around 1 billion people. The 18–24-year-old age group is the largest of the demographics. Overall, there's a mostly even split between the genders with 51 per cent female and 49 per cent male. (Sproutsocial, 2020).

Because Instagram has been around for nearly a decade and has become increasingly influential, it boasts a global user audience. The highest concentration of users is in the US at 116 million users. Next, is India at 73 million users and Brazil at 72 million users. In the next few years, the international user market will soon surpass the US user base. This means there's plenty of opportunities for international brands to market to their consumers.

Pinterest

Pinterest is a social media platform that allows its users to post and share pictures featuring different brands. This can be most attractive and appealing to brands that depend on visual imagery in the promotion of the brand. It has an easy-to-create 'Buy It' pins on products, as well as its ability to generate more referral traffic than other forms of social media. The company makes its money from promoted pins.

Since its formation in 2010, Pinterest has achieved phenomenal growth in terms of users and market value. As at October 2020, Pinterest stats include the following (Omnicore Agency, 2020):

- 94 per cent of social media marketers are using Pinterest and 144.5 million people can be reached with adverts on Pinterest
- It has total number of active users of 416 million and the average number of monthly searches is 2 billion
- Largest Pinterest user base outside of the USA is Germany with 146 million users and some 50 per cent of users reside outside the USA
- 85 per cent of Pinners use their mobile App and the average duration of Pinterest visit is five minutes. 50 per cent of users have made a purchase after seeing a promoted pin
- The total number of Pinterest pins is 240 billion, the total number of boards is 4 billion and holidays is the most popular search category
- 90 per cent of weekly Pinners make their purchase decisions on Pinterest and 77 per cent of weekly Pinners have discovered a new product on Pinterest. Pins that show a customer using a product are 67 per cent more likely to drive offline sales lift
- Females represent 71 per cent of its user base and 35 per cent of users are aged between 18 and 29 and the median age for users is 40
- 70 per cent of users have college degrees, earn an average income of $62,500 and
- Its market value is estimated to be $25 billion

However, Pinterest suffers from the limitation of being more focused on its niche content, particularly lifestyle content, and tends to cater more for a female audience.

TikTok

Since its launch in early 2018, TikTok has been covered by seemingly every major publication and has racked up millions of downloads globally. Despite TikTok's major early success, the app still feels like a bit of a mystery, especially to marketers. In fact, until recently, its parent company, ByteDance, has not disclosed many metrics at all. In its first year, all we really knew was that an odd-ball video app was going viral, topping global app store charts, and gaining a huge fan base from Gen-Z. TikTok now offers five advertising tiers aimed at big brands. One of which, a branded hashtag challenge, reportedly costs $150,000 per day (Digiday, 2019).

When making decisions about your social strategy, marketers are probably more interested in numbers than viral capabilities as proof of an app's staying power.

- Within TikTok's first year, it reportedly reached 500 million monthly active users. TikTok reports having over 800 million monthly active users worldwide by October 2019
- Musical.ly, a lip-syncing app which ByteDance purchased and merged with TikTok, reportedly had 100 million monthly active users when it was purchased by TikTok in 2018.
- Douyin, TikTok's original standalone app in China, had 300 million users at the time Musical.ly merged with TikTok.
- As of early 2019, TikTok is the third-most downloaded app globally.
- By February 2019, TikTok hit 1 billion downloads, beating Instagram and Facebook in app stores.
- As of late October 2019, TikTok was the Top Free App in the Entertainment section of the Apple App Store.

Demographics

While TikTok's user base is dominated by Gen-Z in the United States, many millennials have adopted it around the world. And, although it might feel like TikTok is huge in the US, the app's biggest audience is in China, where the platform is called Douyin. Here's a breakdown of TikTok's major demographic stats (MarketingCharts, 2020).

- Roughly 50 per cent of TikTok's global audience is under the age of 34 with 26 per cent between 18 and 24.

- Just over one in eight adults have joined TikTok
- 56 per cent of TikTok users are male.
- TikTok is now available in 155 countries.
- Over 500 million of TikTok's monthly active users are Chinese.
- The app has 26.5 million monthly active users in the U.S
- 60 per cent of TikTok's US audience is between the ages of 16 and 24.

User Behaviour

- TikTok is a fast-paced app. The second you log in, you see a video at the top of a feed that's algorithmically curated around your interests. If you enjoy the video you're watching, you can follow, comment, and like the content directly from the video post. If you're not loving what you see, you can keep swiping in an upward motion to immediately see more odd videos.
- TikTok can easily lead viewers to spend more time than expected watching an endless stream of often comedic videos. Since these videos are usually between 15 seconds and one minute, it makes the app ideal for people who need quick entertainment on their morning commute or when they're bored at home.
- Because of TikTok's quick pace and entertainment factor, the stats below aren't that surprising:
  - The average user spends 52 minutes per day on TikTok.
  - 90 per cent of TikTok users visit the app more than once per day.
  - Users open the app eight times per day on average.
  - TikTok claims that the average session is nearly five minutes, which is longer than Snapchat or Instagram's.

Viral Trends and Influencers on TikTok

- Like YouTube, Vine, Instagram, as well as other past and present video apps, TikTok has opened doors for influencers, comedians, meme creators and even some brands. While it's still a bit too early to see how successful its influencers and trends will be in the long run, here are a few interesting tidbits:

- The most followed individual on TikTok is a comedic poster and influencer named Loren Gray. She has 34.4 million followers. (TikTok)
- One of the earliest branded hashtag challenges was Guess' #InMyDenim challenge. According to TikTok, videos marked with this hashtag have received a grand total of 38.8 million views. (TikTok)
- Rapper Lil Nas X credits the success of his song 'Old Town Road' to TikTok. The song was propelled to #1 on the Billboard Top 100 in 2019 after the artist uploaded it to TikTok.

The practice and adoption of social media is now a global phenomenon and the techniques explained earlier can be applied in most parts of the world. However, China is a notable exception due to government restrictions. Social media platforms such as Facebook, YouTube and Twitter are banned in China despite the growing popularity of social media. As a consequence, many Chinese owned and operated social media platforms have emerged in recent years including the following:

- Weibo – which is a micro-blogging platform and is deemed a combination of Facebook and Twitter. Its users will typically use it to upload videos and images, follow individuals and read posts. Weibo has an active user base of over 313 million and is most popular in big cities and towns.
- QQ – is a messaging application that offers users many features such as games, shopping, group chats and voice chat. It has a user base of over 869 million
- Youku – is the video sharing version of YouTube in China. It mainly offers users streamed or downloaded movies and television shows and allows brands to appeal to their target audiences via banner advertisements, branded viral videos and pause advertisements. It has a user base of over 580 million.
- Baidu Tieba – offers a communication platform that is tightly connected with the search engine services of Baidu. It has over 660 million active monthly users and more importantly it offers businesses and brands the ability and opportunity to create their own forums that users can be directed to base on searches of the brand name on the search engine.

The growth of digital marketing and social media has created a new era with many distinct needs. These trends portend changes that need to be made in how marketers organize their marketing efforts and more importantly deliver value to their customers. There is now a wide variety of marketing communication options and the availability of data to target customers with offerings at the right time and place. This makes it possible for marketers to better engage with customers.

However, despite the huge benefits that marketers can leverage from adopting and implementing social media marketing, it is worth noting that social media marketing presents challenges as well. These challenges include the following:

- Firms may find it difficult to gauge precisely what the Return On Investment (ROI) is when using social media
- Concerns over privacy may necessitate further legislation preventing the use of customer information for advertising targeting
- Audiences may be too distracted to pay attention especially with the huge volumes of advertisements they see daily
- Competition for certain key words can drive up marketing budgets
- Lack of control over advertisement placement can be potentially harmful and viewed as a spam
- Non-visual content (text only) advertisement type can limit what the brand can convey

The digital era has tremendously shifted consumer behaviours in significant ways and these changes are critical because they assist in highlighting the shifts taking place in marketing and brand management. Therefore, marketers have to also evolve and develop strategies to address these changes in advertising spending across a broad range of digital channels. This calls for an organizational structure and processes that support the marketing strategy adopted by the firm. Based on the aforementioned limitations of social media marketing, it becomes imperative for firms and specifically marketers to carefully analyse plan, implement, monitor and measure social media activities. As such, there are a number of factors that must be taken into consideration when developing a successful strategy that can contribute towards the firm's achievement of its marketing objectives.

- The senior management of the company should develop an understanding of how products and brands are being researched and viewed online and how consumers are using these channels to research their products.

- Cross-functional coordination between the different departments within the organization is increasingly important for a faster decision-making process and problem solving in a much more integrated manner

- Data-driven decision-making will become more important and a standard operating procedure. Organizations should strive and compete to gain the best data available and more importantly, to use it in the most effective manner

- The marketing strategy should be viewed as part of an overall strategy exercise that involves understanding how data is collected, used and shared within the organization

- By acquiring relevant and up-to-date data about what types of customers are interested in which products, which digital or social media channels they access information about the product and can personalize a given message to the target audience based on their behaviours. It is also critical for marketers to gain an understanding and appreciation of how a brand's appeal shifts across the different stages of the consumer decision-making.

- Marketers also need to gain a solid understanding and appreciation of how online and offline communications interact and coordinating an online digital channel strategy is also critical. This is because even within digital channels, there are many options that go beyond just social media marketing, including e-mail marketing, search and banner advertising, the brand website and so on.

Factors to Consider when Choosing Advertising Media

- Cost of media
- The target market or audience
- Control or measurability of media
- Media availability
- Reach or coverage of the medium
- Media used by competitors
- The nature of the product to be advertised
- Lead time to produce and feature the advertisement

Developing Advertising Campaigns

It is essential to create an outline of what goals an advertising campaign should achieve, how to accomplish those goals and how to determine whether the campaign was successful. Developing an advertising plan ensures that your marketing budgets will be spent wisely to target the right audience. A fine-tuned advertising plan is the key to increasing awareness of your business, products and services, regardless of the size or type of your company. An advertising campaign is an attempt to reach a particular target market by designing a series of advertisements and placing them in various media.

Process or Steps in Developing Advertising Campaigns

To develop and implement an advertising campaign, follow these general steps:

1) Identify and analyse the target audience
2) Define the advertising objectives
3) Determine the advertising budget
4) Develop the media plan
5) Create the advertising message
6) Execute the campaign
7) Evaluate the effectiveness of the advertising campaign

Identify and Analyse Target Audience

The advertising target is the group of people at whom the advertisements are aimed. Information that is commonly needed includes:

- Age
- Income
- Ethnic origin
- Gender
- Education
- Lifestyles and interests
- Media habits
- Buying behaviours

Specify and Define Advertising Objectives

The advertising objectives will specify what the organization wants to achieve from the campaign. The SMART criteria should guide the setting of the objectives.

Examples of advertising objectives may include:

- Creating brand awareness
- Educating consumers about the product
- Changing consumer attitudes
- Inducing product trial and sales

Determine Advertising Budget

The budget specifies the total amount of money that the organization allocates for advertising over a period. Factors affecting the budgetary allocation include the following:

- Financial situation (health) of the company
- Size of the market
- Type of product being advertised
- Target market – B2B or B2C
- Level of competition in the market

Methods for Setting Advertising Budgets

There are several methods for setting the campaign budgets:

- **Percentage of sales** involves allocating a percentage of the company's overall sales to be spent on executing the marketing plan.
- **Competitive parity** implies fixing marketing expenditure in relation to the expenditure incurred by competitors.
- **All-you-can-afford** is a crude and unscientific but commonly used method. The firm simply takes a view on what it thinks it can afford to spend on marketing.
- **The objective and task method** implies that marketing objectives are set and then the tasks needed to accomplish them are identified. Estimating the cost of these tasks then sets the budget. This is the most scientific method but can be difficult and time consuming.
- **Historical basis** implies that the marketing communications budget is based on the knowledge and previous experiences of the key managers. Year-on-year figures provide the basis for following trends and making decisions accordingly. The danger of adopting this method is that communication costs do not remain constant.
- **Arbitrary method** implies that senior managers in the company will use their experiences and knowledge to determine the budget.

Develop a Media Plan

The media plan specifies the exact media vehicles to be used for the advertising campaign and the dates and times when the advertisements will be shown. The choice of media vehicle depends on such factors as:

- Cost
- Reach
- Frequency
- Type of product advertised
- Choice of target market
- Lead times
- Communication effectiveness

Marketers use a **Cost Comparison Indicator** to enable them to compare the cost media vehicles in relation to the number of people reached by each vehicle.

Advertising Media Scheduling

Scheduling refers to the pattern of advertising timing, represented as plots on a yearly flowchart. These plots indicate the pattern of scheduled times that coincide with favourable selling periods. The classic scheduling models are continuity, flighting and pulsing.

Continuity

This model is primarily for non-seasonal products and some seasonal products. Advertising runs steadily with little variation over a campaign period. There may be short gaps at regular intervals and also long gaps – for instance, one ad every week for throughout the year, and then a pause before the cycle picks up again. This pattern of advertising is prevalent in service and packaged goods that require continuous reinforcement on the audience for top of mind recollection at point of purchase.

Advantages of Continuity Scheduling:

- Works as a regular reminder.
- Covers the entire purchase cycle.
- Cost efficiencies in the form of large media discounts.
- Positioning advantages within media.
- Program or plan that identifies the media channels used in an advertising campaign, and specifies insertion or broadcast dates, positions and duration of the messages.

Flighting

In media scheduling for seasonal product categories, flighting involves intermittent and irregular periods of advertising, alternating with shorter periods of no advertising at all. Halloween costumes, for example, are rarely purchased except during the months of September and October.

Advantages of Flighting Scheduling:

- Advertisers buy heavier weight than competitors for a relatively shorter period of time.
- Little waste, since advertising concentrates on the most effective purchasing cycle period.
- Series of commercials can appear as a unified campaign on different media vehicles.

Pulsing Scheduling

Pulsing combines flighting and continuous scheduling by using a low advertising level all year round and heavy advertising during peak selling periods. Product categories that are sold year round but which experience a surge in sales at intermittent periods are good candidates for pulsing. For instance, underarm deodorants sell all year, but will be busier during the summer months.

Advantages of Pulsing Scheduling:

- Covers different market situations.
- Advantages of both continuity and flighting possible.

Factors Affecting Advertising Scheduling

The allocation of advertising expenditure/frequency over time depends on the advertising objectives, nature of the product, type of target customers, distribution channel and other relevant marketing factors. But, mostly, the following five factors are considered when deciding on the timing pattern:

1) **Buyer Turnover** shows the rate at which new buyers enter the market. The rule is, the higher the rate of buyer turnover, the more continuous the advertisement should be.

2) **Purchase Frequency** shows the number of times during the specific period that the average buyer buys the product. The common rule is, the higher the purchase frequency, the more continuous the advertisement should be.

3) **Forgetting Rate** shows the rate at which the buyer forgets the brand. The rule is, the higher the forgetting rate, the more continuous the advertisement should be.

4) **Financial Condition of Company** shows the ability of a company to spend for advertising. The rule is, the more is the ability to spend, the more continuous the advertising will be.

5) **Level of Competition.** Company facing a severe market competition will opt for more continuous advertising through multiple media. The rule is, the more intense the competition, the higher the frequency of advertising will be.

Create Advertising Message

The basic content and form of a brand-advertising message are a function of several factors such as:

- Product features
- Product uses
- Product benefits
- Target markets characteristics
- Advertising campaign objectives
- Choice of advertising media

Types of Advertising Messages

There are two types of advertising messages – emotional based and information/rational based.

1) **Emotional based messages** are intended to touch on the heart strings of consumers and focuses more on how the product 'makes you feel'. Such messages can be in the form of music, sex, fear, fantasy, etc.

- **Fear.** The suggestion of physical danger or social rejection might be alleviated by using the brand, such as the comfort offered by smoking cigarettes.
- **Humour.** Attention and mood can be maintained by relaxing the target audience. Using humor in marketing is a tried and tested strategy for brands to ensure that brand campaigns are impactful and remain memorable for audiences. An example is KFC:FCK – at the beginning of 2018 after KFC changed its supplier, the fast food chain faced nationwide chicken shortages in England, which led to store closures. This of course merited a huge backlash from customers on social media. In response, KFC in the UK took out full-page apologies in the *Sun* and *Metro* newspapers. The clever play on the KFC lettering implied the word 'fuck', by way of apology for the chicken restaurant's massive cock-up. The ad went viral on social media, proving that clever and humorous handling of a PR disaster could heal any number of problems for a business.
- **Animation**. Animation can be memorable, attract attention and in some cases be used to convey complex products in a novel manner. An example would be using cartoon characters when advertising to children.
- **Sex** is used primarily to attract attention and to be salient – for example, perfume, lingerie and weight loss brands tend to use sex appeal, however subliminally, in their advertising messages.
- **Music** provides campaign continuity and a degree of differentiation through recognition as in adverts. The brand Sun Drop used music by the famous rap musician Snoop Dog in its advertisements.

2) **Information or Rational-based messages** are fact-based messages and focus on 'what the product does'. Such messages can be in the form of product comparison with the firm's competitors, technical or scientific competences, or testimonial or endorsements from experts.

- **Factual**. The benefits are presented using reasoned, factual arguments, as for nicotine patches.

- **Slice of life**. Allows the target customer to identify with the characters and a common problem. The brand is then perceived as a suitable solution – detergents can be a good example.
- **Demonstration**. Show the audience how the product solves a problem – floor cleaners, for example, with floors shown before and after use.
- **Comparative**: Through comparison, it is possible to achieve enhanced status and superiority, as for credit and charge cards.

Execute Advertising Campaign

The execution of an advertising campaign requires an extensive amount of planning and coordination. Regardless of whether or not an organization uses an advertising agency, many people and organizations are involved in the actual execution of a campaign.

Implementation requires detailed schedules to ensure that various phases of the work are conducted in conjunction and on time. In some instances, changes may have to be made during the campaign in the light of new circumstances or fast-moving events, to ensure that it better meets the objectives, better satisfies the client managers or better responds to consumer research feedback.

Evaluate/Measure the Effectiveness or Results of the Advertising Campaign

Evaluation is necessary to determine whether stated campaign objectives are met or not. There are various ways to evaluate the effectiveness of advertising campaigns – before, during and after the campaign.

- **Pre-tests**: Evaluations performed before an advertising campaign that attempt to assess the effectiveness of the message.
- **Post-test**: Evaluation of the campaign effectiveness afterwards.
- **Consumer focus groups** are semi-structured discussions led by a moderator involving actual and potential buyers who are asked to judge

the various facets of the advertisement. Such focus groups are used before, during and after a campaign to monitor changes in consumer perceptions. Additionally, the following indicators can be used to assess campaign effectiveness:

- **Sales levels**
- **Customer enquiries levels**

Sales Promotions

These are numerous short-term incentives aimed at generating sales or encouraging consumers to trial the company's products. Such sales promotions can be targeted at

- customers
- intermediaries such as retailers
- distributors and manufacturers
- end-user customers

It is by far the most popular promotion method used by firms offering packaged goods, and accounts for as much as over 50 per cent of their marketing budgets. The popularity of sales promotions as a technique can be attributed to internal pressures on marketing managers to grow sales, aggressive competition in the marketplace and customers becoming familiar with, and thus always expecting, such deals.

The debate rages about the effectiveness and implications of sales promotions. Some commentators argue that their use undermines the brand value and sets up customers to expect such promotions in their future buying decisions (the law of effect). On the other hand, it can be argued that it has minimal negative effects on the brand and actually adds to the brand value over time, especially if price-discounting techniques are not used as part of sales promotions exercises.

What is not in dispute is the rapid and continuous growth in the adoption of sales promotions. This growth can be explained by the following reasons.

- **The need for accountability**
  - Companies focus on immediate profits and sales promotion goes a long way to satisfying this drive.
  - Advertising tends to work in the long term rather than short term. Hence the need to undertake sales promotions to drive sales in the short term
  - Traditional media costs have also escalated to the point where practical alternatives need to be considered.
  - It is relatively easy to measure sales promotion outcomes.
- **Consumer factors**
  - Reduces the risk of purchase
  - Consumers are less loyal to brands
  - Consumers expect constant short-term price cuts
  - Promotions encourage brand switching and helps gain market share
  - Parity products: promotion is the most effective strategy for increasing sales when products are largely undifferentiated
  - Power of the retailer: dominant retailers such as Walmart and Tesco demand incentives to offer shelf space

Employing sales promotions as a marketing technique should start with the identification and specification of the objectives to be attained from such exercises. The objectives of sales promotion include:

- Increasing brand awareness
- Increasing the trial and adoption of new and existing products
- Attracting customers to switch brands from competitors
- Smoothing out fluctuations in demand and supply
- Increasing brand usage
- Boosting customer loyalty

- Disseminating information
- Invigorating mature brands that may be experiencing a decline in sales
- Moving excess stock
- Encouraging retailers to stock the product
- Disrupting the competition
- Generating publicity for the brand
- Enabling the firm to build a database of customers for future marketing exercises.

In developing a sales promotions campaign, marketers must also factor in the following considerations:

- The nature or size of the incentives to be offered – the larger the sales promotions incentive, the more likely that customer participation will increase and subsequent sales will rise.
- The conditions for customer participation – for example, is a purchase necessary to participate or will it be open to everyone or only a targeted segment of the market?
- The duration of the promotion – how long will it last?
- Strategies for promotion and the distribution of the promotion – this may include price discount coupons on the actual product sold in stores or price discounts on online purchases.
- Evaluation – measuring the results against previously defined objectives.

Sales Promotions Techniques

The choice of sales promotion technique will depend on both the firm and product. There are specific sales promotions techniques that can be targeted at both end user consumers and retailers respectively:

- Vouchers
- Buy One Get One Free (BOGOF)
- Price discounts

- Free samples
- Competitions and raffles
- Coupons
- More for less (three for two)
- Loyalty bonuses
- Point of sale displays
- Cause-related promotions – the firm allocates a percentage of sales income to social causes.

For retailers and other B2B customers, manufacturing firms can offer the following sales promotions tactics:

- Volume discounts
- Flexible payment plans
- Returns of unsold stock
- Offer of sample products
- Price discounts
- Trade in – firm allows customers to exchange the old product with a discount for a newer product version
- Offer of promotional merchandise such as key rings, stationery, clothing, water bottles, etc.

Evaluation of Sales Promotions

The effectiveness or otherwise of a sales promotions campaign can be determined using any or a combination of the following:

- Consumer audits to indicate trial rate, repeat purchase
- Sales analysis comparing sales before and after promotions
- Retail audits to track stock turnovers, market during and after promotion
- Voucher/coupon redemption can be coded to help with measuring results
- In-home penetration (pantry checks)

Direct Marketing

Direct marketing is an interactive system of marketing, which uses one or more advertising media to effect a measurable response at any location. If properly applied, direct marketing has the advantage of customizing targeted messages to identified customers and can help in developing customer engagement, brand communities and sales generation.

The growth in the adoption and practice of direct marketing can be explained by the following factors:

- Media fragmentation
- Audience fragmentation
- The cost of above the line advertising
- The importance of narrow casting
- The importance of 'plastic' (credit and debit cards)
- The growth of the service economy
- New technologies (the Internet, computer costs and battery life)
- Change in market information (electronic point of sales)
- The desire for shopping convenience
- Increased competition

The objectives of DM include:

- Dissemination of information
- Generation of sales leads
- Generation of trial leads
- Building relationships with customers

Direct Marketing Techniques

- **Telemarketing** involves the use of telephone services to sell the firm's products directly to consumers. It can target specific demographics or consumers and is widely used in many countries, such as the United States and United Kingdom. However, if not managed properly, it can create a high level of consumer annoyance and many countries have legislation in place to regulate the use of telemarketing.

- **Direct Response TV** involves firms showing advertisements for short periods and then, at the end of the advertisements, displaying contact numbers or website addresses for consumers to call or log onto and order the product advertised. The QVC channel is well known for this approach.
- **Direct mail** involves sending offers and other relative communication messages via letters, brochures, videos or product samples to the addresses of selected consumers. This technique can be very tailored or personalized and can easily be measured in terms of its effectiveness and results.
- **Direct catalogues** takes advantage of the explosion in Internet connectivity to send electronic catalogues showing products offered as well as how to order these.
- **SMS** is a technique becoming very popular due to the explosion in mobile phone usage. It involves the firm sending direct promotional messages to customer's mobile phones with the intention of informing, convincing and prompting them to take action to engage with the firm and potentially buy its products.
- **Kiosk marketing** involves firms displaying information and ordering machines in prominent locations such as airports, stores, shopping malls and train stations.

The Internet and Direct and Digital Marketing

The invention of the Internet and the rapid growth in its use for buying and selling products has transformed the practice of direct marketing. Today, direct marketing predominantly takes the form of digital marketing, with both firms and customers increasingly using the Internet to communicate, sell and buy products. This explosion in digital marketing can be attributed to a range of reasons, including:

- Reduced costs associated with accessing the Internet
- The unstoppable rise in the use of mobile phones with Internet access

- Convenience and ease of use – armchair shopping from the comfort of customers' homes
- Access to a huge and diverse range of products
- Relative low cost of selling and buying products, for both firms and customers
- Allows firms the flexibility to adapt and refine their marketing practices at relatively short notice
- Effective in terms of building and developing long-term, mutually beneficial relationships between sellers and buyers

Types of Direct and Digital Marketing Techniques

Traditional forms of direct marketing such as telemarketing, direct mail, catalogue marketing and kiosk usage are still often used by marketers, but most firms prefer to focus more on the adoption and practice of digital marketing techniques such as online marketing, social media marketing and mobile marketing.

The adoption of digital and social media marketing continues to grow at exponential levels and now dominate the practice of direct marketing. Its practice includes the adoption and use of such digital tools as websites, online videos, blogs, emails, mobile advertisements and apps to engage customers through such devices as consumer's computers, smartphones, Internet-ready televisions and tablets, anytime and anywhere.

Online Marketing

Online marketing implies conducting marketing activities through the Internet by means of using the organization's website, online advertisements and promotions, emails, videos and blogs. For most companies, the creation and management of websites is the primary step in conducting online marketing. Such websites should be visually appealing, rich with useful content and easy to navigate to attract and then retain visitors to the website. These websites can be of two types: marketing websites and branded community websites.

Marketing websites are designed with the purpose of interacting with customers in order to convince and motivate them to make a purchase. As ubiquitous as it may be, Amazon is the classic example of a site that adopts this approach.

Branded community websites, on the other hand, are designed to focus not on sales but rather on presenting engaging content that makes customers feel part of the brand and able to connect more easily to it.

Online advertisements

As consumers spend increasing amounts of time visiting and buying from websites – not least as a result of 2020's pandemic - more companies are today moving a considerable share of their marketing activities and marketing budgets online in order to attract and retain visitors, and grow their online sales as a percentage of their overall sales. This has led to almost constant growth of online advertising in the forms of banner ads within social media and search-related advertisements.

Online search advertisements will normally appear on consumers' screens when they are viewing related content: people looking at holiday destinations will see advertisements by Hotels.com, for example.

Search-related advertisements appear when consumers use search engines such as Google, Bing or Yahoo to obtain information online. This accounts for almost half of all advertisements displayed online and works by allowing marketers to 'buy' specific search terms or words, which they will pay for when consumers click through to the site.

Email Marketing

There is now growing use of email marketing as a digital marketing technique in its own right. The use of email marketing allows marketers to send highly personalized messages and offerings to targeted customers. However, it is also worth noting that it suffers from the long-standing problem of being considered spam and also represents an unsolicited invasion of consumer's privacy. To overcome this problem, marketers are now often obliged to use permission-based email marketing, which allows marketers to direct and send messages to customers who have previously indicated their approval for receiving such emails.

Online Videos

It is now very common practice for marketers to post informational video content on popular social media sites such as Facebook and YouTube. The objective is to promote viral marketing, whereby customers go on to share the video with friends and others in their own networks. This makes such marketing tactics cheap and affordable, but also has the added advantage of being seen as 'trusted' content because it has usually been shared by friends and known acquaintances.

The rise of the influencer

Blogs are now almost ubiquitous, with companies, their customers or other individuals posting content on specific topics to dedicated followers online. This has led to a huge rise in influencers, who specialize in sharing their subject matter expertise – whether that be in terms of food, fashion, cosmetics or travel – with followers on social media. Where such influencers are working with specific brands, it can drive traffic, engage consumers, create buzz and be a great source of customer feedback; it is also relatively cheap compared to other social media techniques. However, it suffers from a number of problematic issues, primarily that it can be difficult to control because it is mainly consumer-driven and hence must be continuously and closely monitored.

Mobile Marketing

The decade-long rise in the numbers of people owning smartphones and other portable devices that offer internet connectivity has compelled marketers to embrace the adoption and practice of mobile marketing. Mobile marketing involves marketers sending marketing information and content to consumers via their mobile devices such as smartphones and tablets and this can be done via Apps, SMS, games consoles and social media networks. Considering that people are attached to their smartphones for large parts of the day, it makes for a convenient window-shopping device.

Research on mobile marketing done by Evinex (2020) found the following interesting statistics:

- 80 per cent of smartphone users check their mobile devices within 15 minutes of waking up
- 79 per cent of adult smartphone users have their phones with them for 22 hours a day
- American adults spend three hours a day on their smartphones
- 95 per cent of all paid Google search ad clicks come from mobile devices
- 78 per cent of mobile brand experiences are described as positive
- 71 per cent of marketers believe mobile marketing is core to their business

Marketers are also producing content and information that are specifically tailored for smartphones to provide information on new product launches, promotional offers and product reviews. As a result, mobile marketing can help in the provision of useful information to customers, the building and maintenance of customer engagement, the enhancement of shopping convenience, and the subsequent stimulation of consumer purchases.

In order to develop successful mobile marketing campaigns, it is imperative that firms consider carefully the following:

1) Create content that is mobile friendly
2) Make use of apps and platforms
3) Consider the firms intended or targeted audiences to create effective mobile advertising

The rapid adoption and growth of mobile advertising can be attributed to the numerous benefits it provides to marketers and these benefits include the following:

1) Convenience and engagement as it enables the firm to address its target audiences that it wants to send its advertising messages to and hence build and maintain engagement with such consumers.

2) Simplicity – as it is fairly easy to design mobile marketing campaigns. There are also many advertising agencies that can be outsourced for technical support and software development that is user-friendly.

3) Analytics – makes it possible and easier to track user interactions with mobile advertisements. For example Google Analytics, Countly and Smartlook are examples of software tracking systems that can be used for this purpose.

4) Multi-language – enables firms the possibility of providing advertisements that can be switched to different languages. This makes customers more comfortable with interacting with mobile devices and advertisements.

5) Location-based – this is a feature only available for mobile services and helps the firm's customers receive specific information that is relevant for their location.

6) Wider audience reach because of the huge ownership of mobile devices in almost all parts of the world.

7) Speed – allows for fast and real time communications with audiences.

Consumer's engagement and interactions with the Internet have undergone tremendous shifts and will, continue to evolve with advancements in technologies. Therefore, to maximize the effectiveness of mobile marketing, marketers need to take into account the following pointers:

1) Prioritize on mobile experiences and personalization: marketers should focus on offering consumers the best mobile experiences

in order to engage and retain their loyalty. These experiences should include in-app messaging, product recommendations, individualized customer experiences and other relevant information. These can be achieved by for example, providing different customers with different offers specifically based on their profiles such as age, gender, location etc.

2) Enable mobile shopping from social media – there is no doubt that social media is the best channel available to marketers to engage with customers. Besides there is also growing interest on the part of consumers to interact with companies and brands on their networks. The same principle applies to mobile shopping via social media as it provides customers with the opportunities to feel comfortable to chat and share personal data with the company.

3) Strengthen company's SMS marketing – mobile SMS marketing provides huge benefits to firms especially when compared with the use of emails for example, as the chances of consumers opening their SMS are much higher than with emails. Emails suffer from being considered spam and some consumers do not bother to even open their emails. Most people open their SMS and hence will receive messages from the company and follow through with the desired action. SMS that are personalized tend to be well received by consumers especially when combined with an offer such as mobile coupons.

4) Monitor and study mobile user behaviours – gaining an understanding of customers is an important prerequisite to success marketing. A great deal of customer data can be gleaned from their engagement with mobile devices especially via the company's apps and social media and such data can then be gathered, analysed and acted upon.

5) Focus on SEO efforts for mobile – Mobile SEO is mandatory and marketers need to optimize content to achieve better rankings on SERPs. The number of people using their mobile devices to search for information is growing rapidly and such mobile searches can

help with sales of the company's products and services. As such, marketers must focus on the company's SEO efforts and also track performances to help in determining the amount of traffic generated from mobile devices. This is also critical for gaining customer engagement and hence the key is to ensure that the company's site and content are optimized for mobile users.

6) Update Company's strategy with the latest trends and technology – Technologies continue to evolve and impact on people's lives at fast rates. It is also the same with mobiles which have also gone through unprecedented changes as consumers now use them for almost everything. Therefore, marketers need to be aware of the latest trends and more importantly, to develop appropriate strategies that match such advancements in technology.

Evaluation of Direct Marketing

- Response rate – counting the number of responses to a mailshot
- Conversion rate – the number of responses that lead to confirmed orders
- Order value
- Cost per enquiry or order
- Hits on the websites – the number of people who visit the website as a result of being redirected from a specific online advertisement.

Personal Selling

Personal selling implies the employment of a sales force to market a company's offerings to its customers or potential customers. It is also the oldest form of marketing communications and is considered the most effective communication technique for building, developing and maintaining customer relationships. Classic examples of organizations that adopt the use of personal selling include charities such as the Red Cross or Save the Children, for which personal selling is a key component of their fundraising activities.

Depending on the size and nature of the firm's business, it can organize its sales force in terms of geographical territory, product category, or customer or industry lines. It is important when developing a sales force strategy to include consideration for such critical issues as structure, recruitment, training, compensation, supervision and evaluation of sales force performances.

The functions of the sales force can include:

- Order taking from customers
- Order delivery to customers
- Marketing research or information gathering, which can be shared internally to respond to any changes happening in the marketplace
- Sales or leads generation, which can then be converted into sales
- Relationship building with customers to ensure and achieve loyalty
- Product demonstration to potential buyers
- Providing aftersales services to customers
- Handling customer complaints

The Personal Selling Process

- **Prospecting and qualifying** – the first step of the personal selling process involves identifying and determining consumers who could potentially be customers. Personal selling is time-consuming and expensive, so it is critical that any support helps the salespeople to focus their efforts on the best leads and prospects. Such prospects can be identified via referrals from existing customers or through captured consumer enquiries via phone, email or social media.
- **Pre-approach** – this step of the process involves the salesperson doing their homework on the prospect, prior to making any kind of contact. This will allow the salesperson to better understand the prospect's needs, determine the best time to schedule any visit or follow-up call, and decide on the overall sales strategy to be adopted when interacting with the prospect.
- **Presentation and demonstration** – this is the most critical stage of the selling process, when the salesperson should focus on presenting and

explaining the product's (or service's) value proposition to the prospect. This means that the salesperson needs to be able to articulate how the product solves the prospective customer's particular needs. Hence, the presentation should focus on understanding those needs and exactly how the firm's products can address and solve them.

- **Overcoming objections** – it can be expected that most customers will have some objections following the salesperson's presentation. Such customer objections could be about the price, delivery schedules, order quantities, the design of the product or its aftersales service. It is important at this stage for the salesperson to allow the customer to talk, to clarify and explain objections and ensure that they feel heard while also providing the most effective answers and solutions to such objections. Overcoming any customer objections will make it easier to move the customer to the next stage of the process – closing the sale.

- **Closing the sale** – once any customer objections have been handled, the salesperson should work to close the sale by asking the customer to place orders, review and sign the contract, or by offering any additional incentives that will motivate the customer to confirm the order at that particular moment.

- **Follow-up and maintenance** – this stage is important because the placing of just one order should never be the end of the salesperson/customer relationship. In terms of best practice, the salesperson should contact the customer to ensure that delivery of the product has arrived and providing any additional assistance required by the customer. This will form the foundation for building, developing and maintaining a long-term mutually beneficial relationship between the salesperson and the customer.

Evaluation of Personal Selling

- Productivity – sales levels
- Account development levels
- Expenses incurred in acquiring customers

Sponsorship

This is when an organization undertakes to carry the cost of hosting an event in return for advertising space and brand awareness. It is therefore an investment in cash or in-kind activity, in return for access to the exploitable commercial potential associated with this activity. It provides the company with a platform to promote its interests and brands by tying them to a specific and meaningfully related event or cause.

Sponsorship has seen a surge in its adoption as a marketing communications tool. This is in part because of the huge explosion in the number of global televised events and in part because people are devoting more time in pursuit of leisurely activities such as watching sporting events (now sponsored by, say, Nike or Adidas). If applied effectively, sponsorship can help in creating high levels of brand awareness, even though it might not necessarily lead to more customer trial or purchase of the firm's products. However, it should not be used in isolation but needs the support of other marketing communication activities such as sales promotions, advertising and public relations.

The objectives of sponsorship include:

- Increasing brand awareness and generating publicity
- Building and enhancing corporate image
- Raising awareness of brands related to products restricted in advertising through various legislation, such as alcohol (it should be noted that tobacco-related sponsorship was banned a number of years ago)
- Building good corporate citizenship within global and local communities
- Motivating employees to feel proud to work for the organization based on its positive corporate reputation
- Changing people's perceptions of the brand

Types of Sponsorship

It is crucial that there is a good fit between the event sponsored and the product to be featured during the event.

- **Event sponsorship** – sponsorship of major events such as the Olympic games, World Cup or Formula One
- **Programme sponsorship** – sponsorship of television or radio programmes
- **Person sponsorship** – Nike sponsor the best athletes in different sports
- **Cause-related sponsorship** – This is philanthropic in nature and includes sponsorship of social causes
- **Art sponsorship** – sponsorship of musicians, art houses and artists – e.g., BP's support for the National Portrait Gallery in London (although this brings its own problems in terms of regular demonstrations against the use of money from fossil fuels to promote the arts)

Evaluation of Sponsorship

- Media exposure measurement – amount of media coverage achieved
- Pre-testing and post-testing of awareness in relation to sponsorship activity
- Feedback from participants – from customers, sponsored parties and other stakeholders
- Effect on corporate image

Public Relations

Public relations are planned and sustained efforts on the part of an organization to create goodwill and a positive public perception in the minds of the public. Public relations is therefore the management of relationships between the organization and its stakeholders with the objective of promoting and protecting the firm's image and reputation. Its goal is to achieve planned and sustained efforts to establish and maintain goodwill and mutual understanding between an organization and its public.

An organization's public or stakeholders include:

- Customers
- Employees
- Financial institutions
- Shareholders
- A local community
- Central government
- The media
- Pressure groups

Objectives of Public Relations

- To create and maintain the corporate and brand image
- To enhance the position and standing of the organization in the eyes of the public
- To communicate the organization's ethos, corporate values and philosophy
- To disseminate information to the public
- To undertake damage limitation exercises to overcome poor or negative publicity for the company
- To raise company profile and forge stronger, longer-lasting customer and supply chain relationships.

Ultimately, PR is undertaken to shape the public's perceptions and attitudes towards the company.

From		To
- Negative	➜	Positive
- Hostility	➜	Sympathy
- Prejudice	➜	Acceptance
- Apathy	➜	Interest
- Ignorance	➜	Knowledge

Public Relations Techniques

- **Press releases**: This is a written document prepared by an organization for the media – also called the press – with the aim of making a newsworthy announcement such as the launch of a new product, new hires, corporate partnerships, new investment from investors, financial performance or new awards received. The press release is normally one to three pages in length as is disseminated and shared with media reporters and editors so that it can be featured in media outlets such as television stations, newspapers, magazines or websites.

- **Press conferences**: This is an event organized by the organization to officially distribute information and address questions from the media. Typically, press conferences are announced and hosted in relation to specific public relations issues such as new product launches, major personnel changes, unveiling of a new production facility or when crisis happens. Corporate press conferences are generally led by the company's executive management or a press liaison or communications officer. It provides the company with the opportunity to present and convey positive news stories to the media and hence gain favourable media exposure, greater brand recognition and authority in the market at a significantly lower cost than running an advertising campaign.

- **Annual reports**: These are yearly financial statements that are published by corporations and shared with investors and other stakeholders such as the media. It allows the company to show evidence of its financial performances over the past year as well as future financial projections. Most companies, however, view their annual report as a potentially effective marketing tool to disseminate their perspective on company fortunes. With this in mind, many medium-sized and large companies devote large sums of money to making their annual reports as attractive and informative as possible. In such instances the annual report becomes a forum through which a company can relate, influence, preach, opine and discuss any number of issues and topics.

- **Lobbying**: This is an aspect of public relations which is generally undertaken to influence public opinions, policies and laws. People who work in lobbying professions are called lobbyists and they work directly with elected officials to promote and fight against issues beneficial or detrimental to their clients. In the US for example, E-Cigarette manufacturers are making use of lobbyists to fight state proposal to ban sale of such products near high schools. Most firms appoint external lobbyists but in some giant corporations, they can have an internal lobbying team with the PR department.

- **Media relations**: Media relations involves working with the media for the purpose of informing the public of an organization's mission, policies and practices in a positive, consistent and credible manner. Typically, this means coordinating directly with the people responsible for producing the news and features in the mass media. The goal of media relations is to maximize positive coverage in the mass media without paying for it directly through advertising.
- **Events hosting**: These are fun ways to garner the attention of the media and involves hosting a launch party to celebrate a specific corporate event such as after the launch of a new product. Many firms now host post-product launch parties where targeted audiences such as celebrities and the media for example are invited to celebrate and the intention of such parties is to create a buzz that people will talk about for some time to come.
- **Product launches**: This implies the firm creating a buzz when new product are being launched into the market. The media houses will be invited to cover such stories with the aim of generating publicity for the firm and new product being launched.
- **Facility visits**: This involves the firm opening its doors and welcoming visitors to tour its premises or production facilities. Such visitors includes the media. Often, firms promote facility visits when such new facilities are built or in response to a negative press coverage. By opening its doors, it shows the public via media houses the prevailing situation to promote or counter stories accordingly.
- **Donations and charitable giving**: The firm will provide support and allocate a percentage of its profits to charitable organizations.

Organizations often realize positive results by fostering strong relations with important and potentially influential audiences, such as members of their local community. Programs that are supportive of the community include: sponsoring local organizations and institutions (e.g., arts organizations, community activities, and parks); conducting educational workshops (e.g., for teachers and parents); and donating product or money in support of community events. Effective community relations can help a company weather bad publicity or a crisis situation that can unexpectedly arise due to such issues as problems with a product, perceived service shortcomings, unethical behaviour by management and false rumour. Some companies also make an effort to contribute to charitable groups, especially organizations that have some relationship to the company's mission.

- **Cause-related marketing**: This refers to strategic positioning and marketing tool which links a company or brand to a relevant social cause or issue for mutual benefit, unlike corporate philanthropy which involves specific donations that are tax deductible. It typically involves the company collaborating with charitable organizations to provide support to such organization such as charities. For example, the French Mineral water brand Evian donates a percentage of its product sales to charities that provide drinking water to refuges. Such corporate activities are very powerful in generating positive brand image in the minds of consumers and society at large.

Crisis Public Relations

A key function of PR will be to handle crisis situations such as poor financial performance or annual results, scandals relating to senior management, or accidents. Factors leading to the rise in the importance of crisis management as a specific discipline within the world of PR include issues such as:

- The rise in consumer groups
- The speed with which information can be disseminated globally

- The rate of advances in technology
- Changes in the economic environment (globalization or increased competition, for example, can lead firms into crisis)
- Uncertainty surrounding acts of terrorism of incidents of conflict.

Managing PR in a Crisis

Managing a crisis is possible, but it requires discipline. A crisis is a significant threat to the company's operations that can have detrimental and negative consequences if not handled properly. In crisis management, the threat is the potential damage a crisis can inflict on an organization, its stakeholders and an industry. Typically, a crisis can create three related threats: (1) public safety, (2) financial loss and (3) reputation loss. Some crises, such as industrial accidents and product harm, can result in injuries and even loss of lives. Crises can create financial loss by disrupting operations, creating a loss of market share/purchase intentions, or spawning lawsuits related to the crisis. As such, it is imperative that marketers and companies adopt and follow the process outlined below as part of the crisis management process.

- Designate a single spokesperson to be the face of the company. This implies that all communications emanating from the company will be presented by the designated spokesperson
- Tell your story first and strive to be open and honest with the information available. By being proactive with communicating the story, the firm will be more trusted and credible as opposed to taking a reactive stance.
- Never go 'off the record' – firms should stick to the script and be consistent in their messaging
- Keep your employees informed (avoid rumours spreading internally).
- Stress your company or product's positives. Emphasize on the good things that the company is involved in so as to paint a positive image in the minds of stakeholders

Evaluation of Public Relations

- **Awareness** – through market research
- **Attitude** – attitude change measurement
- **Media coverage and tone** – number of column inches achieved, the types of headings and tone of coverage
- **Positioning** – particularly in relation to competitors
- **Share price** – movements in stock prices (positive or negative effects)
- **Sales** – bad publicity will usually affect sales

The American Alliance of Artists and Audiences

The American Alliance of Artists and Audiences (4A Arts) is a national web platform designed to increase participation in the arts, humanities, sciences, arts education and cultural advocacy across America. All site visitors are free to search the organization's national listings for events, education and advocacy from all disciplines of arts and culture. The organization's website (4AArts.org) features a robust search function designed specifically to serve the arts and cultural sector that allows users to search the site to find programming by location, date, category, type, specialty, diversity focus, accessibility, age appropriateness and 4A Arts Member Benefits.

The organization's listings on its web portal includes the following:

- events and programming such as performances, exhibits/exhibitions, festivals, film/video events, public art, readings, residencies, social events and tours and walks;
- education programmes such as classes, workshops, lectures/talks, school programs, intensives, conferences, seminars, professional development, studio or private instruction, symposiums, residencies and art camps; and
- advocacy initiatives such as actions, events, initiatives, workshops and conferences.

The goal of 4A Arts is to become a centralized resource for arts and cultural programming by artists and organizations of all sizes and from all disciplines across the country. By promoting all disciplines, it hopes to encourage audiences to discover and explore new types of programming. The organization intends to feature education and advocacy initiatives on the same platform as other arts and cultural events, in order to raise awareness of critical connection among education, advocacy and arts and cultural programming. As its membership grows, it plans to work with advocacy organizations to develop strategies to engage its members in their ongoing work, in order to elevate the social, economic and political perception of arts and culture.

4A Arts is funded by contributions and membership fees, which are vital for it to maintain its web platform, expand its information resources, provide free access to search features, and reach out to encourage new artists and organizations to post on its site.

Organizations and Artists

The organization helps arts and cultural groups, presenters, educators, advocates, service organizations and individual artists to achieve their goals by sharing their work and magnifying its value. Organizations and artists can post their events, education programs and advocacy activities on its website for free. It solicits organizations and artists that post on the site to consider offering discounts or other benefits to 4A Arts members. Events and profile pages with discounts show up in discount searches and incentivize members to buy tickets. These discounts will also help 4A Arts to build a national community of users and members, which will in turn help to build audiences for its programming and for arts and culture across the country.

Membership

Individuals can become 4A Arts members by paying a US$25 annual fee. Membership benefits include the following:

- Accessing Discounts and Benefits to Arts and Culture across America: 4A Arts members have access to discounts and other benefits offered by some of the organizations and artists that post on 4AArts.org. Discounts and benefits vary by organization/artist and may include ticket discounts, invitations to special events, and so on.
- Staying Informed with Event Alerts: 4A Arts members also have the option to set up custom email alerts for saved searches and favourite organizations and artists.

Question

4A Arts is a young organization that needs to raise its levels of brand awareness and attract potential customers as members.

Based on the information given in the above case study, recommend and justify the most appropriate marketing communications / promotional tools that 4A Arts can adopt and implement to achieve its marketing objectives of achieving higher levels of brand awareness and increased membership.

CHAPTER THIRTEEN

The Extended Marketing Mix – People, Process and Physical Evidence

As previously explained in the preceding chapters, the extended marketing mix refers to the elements that marketers use in their practice of marketing to meet the expectations and satisfaction of customers. Initially, these marketing mix elements were product, price, place and promotion. However, these have been extended to include people, process and physical evidence and hence the name extended marketing mix. Extending the marketing mix by adding Physical Evidence, Process and People to the usual 4Ps allows us to connect the marketing function much more closely to both human resource management and operations. These additional 3Ps are more relative to the marketing of services, although they can also be present – and are often necessary – in the marketing of physical goods.

The People Mix

People play a crucial role in the production and delivery of products and services. The physical presence of people performing the job is a vital aspect of customer satisfaction. All companies are reliant on the people who run them, from front-line sales staff to the Managing Director. People are therefore an essential ingredient in service provision; recruiting and training the right staff is required to create a competitive advantage. Customers make judgments about service provision and delivery based on the people representing your organization. This is because people are one of the few elements of the service that customers can see and interact with. Having the right people in the right place at the right time and with the right skills is essential because they are as much a part of the business offering as the products and services the firm is offering.

People issues include:

- Staff should dress and appear in a manner that is appropriate
- Employees should have the right attitudes and temperament especially in their dealings with customers
- Employees should display high levels of commitment and dedication in providing services to customers
- Staff should adopt the right behaviours and mannerisms in their interactions with customers
- Employees of the company should also adopt the high standards of professionalism when serving customers
- Employees should possess the right levels of knowledge, skills and competencies so as to better meet the expectations of customers.

It is imperative that marketing managers ensure that people are recruited effectively and managed professionally by means of the following:

- Careful recruitment of staff
- Mindful policies for the selection of staff
- Established programmes for staff training
- Setting standard and consistent operational practices
- Setting standard operational rules
- Adopting and implementing effective motivational programmes
- Setting effective policies of staff reward and remuneration
- Setting consistent and continuous monitoring of staff performances against established organizational criteria

The Process Mix

Process involves the ways in which the marketer's task is achieved. The delivery of the service is usually done with a close connection to the customer (either in person or online), so how the service is delivered is once again part of what the consumer is paying for. In other words, process refers to the ways in which the activities are provided and performed by the firm in its interactions with and servicing of its customers. Thus this element of the marketing mix looks at the systems used to deliver the service. Imagine you walk into Burger King and order a Whopper Meal and you get it delivered within two minutes. What was the process that allowed you to obtain an efficient service delivery? Banks that send out credit cards automatically when their customers' old ones have expired again require an efficient process to identify expiry dates and renewal. An efficient service that replaces old credit cards will foster consumer loyalty and confidence in the company. All services need to be underpinned by clearly defined and efficient processes. This will avoid confusion and promote a consistent service. In other words processes mean that everybody knows what to do and how to do it.

The process mix includes a consideration for the following issues:

- Company policies such as refunds or the return of goods
- Service features such as online ordering and delivery
- Information dissemination and handling
- Mechanization, such as the use of technologies in service deliveries
- Queuing systems in stores

The Physical Evidence Mix

Physical evidence is about where the service is being delivered from. It is particularly relevant to retailers operating out of shops. This element of the marketing mix will distinguish a company from its competitors. Physical evidence can be used to charge a premium price for a service and establish a positive experience. For example all hotels provide a bed to sleep on but one of the things affecting the price charged, is the condition of the room (physical evidence) holding the bed. Customers will make judgments about the organization based on the physical evidence. For example if you walk into a restaurant you expect a clean and friendly environment, if the restaurant is smelly or dirty, customers are likely to walk out. This is before they have even received the service. The physical evidence therefore relates to those aspects of a company that customers can see and feel in order to form an impression of the service or its provider. Almost all services include some physical elements, even if the bulk of what the consumer is paying for is intangible. For example, a hair salon provides their client with a completed haircut and treatment package, while an insurance company gives their customers some form of printed material such as brochures or access to the relevant details on the firm's website.

Examples of physical evidence include the following:

- Logos associated with the brand
- Colours associated with the brand
- Company vehicles
- Labels used on products
- Packaging of products
- Ambience in the stores or offices
- Office layout and decorations
- Paperwork or office stationery used in communications to customers
- Appearance of staff such as uniforms and dressing
- Equipment used in stores, plants or offices

CHAPTER FOURTEEN

Marketing Planning and Strategy

Marketing activities need to be carefully planned, executed and evaluated. A marketing plan should identify and stipulate the set marketing objectives to be achieved and the relative strategies for achieving these predetermined objectives. Planning is necessary in order to:

- Provides a 'road map' for identifying and achieving set objectives and implementing the overall strategy
- Provides a framework for monitoring, feedback and control of planned marketing activities
- Clarifies roles and functions to staff in charge of executing the plan
- Specifies how resources are to be allocated
- Assigns responsibilities to staff and specifies deadlines within which set tasks should be accomplished
- Creates awareness of barriers to achievement of set objectives
- Ensures customer focus and competitor awareness
- Assists efficiency and effectiveness in delivering set objectives and planned marketing activities

Reasons for Planning Failures

- Failure to understand the customer
- Failure to obtain senior management commitment
- Failure to manage the change
- Inability to predict environmental reaction

- Underestimation of time requirements
- Overestimation of resource competence
- Failure to follow or co-ordinate the plan

The Marketing Planning Process

The marketing planning process identifies and explains the steps involved in developing a marketing plan. The typical marketing planning process follows a MAOSTIC Framework:

1) Mission and vision
2) Analysis of the marketing environment
3) Objectives setting
4) Strategy choice and evaluation
5) Tactics
6) Implementation
7) Control

M = Mission and Vision of the Business

The mission defines the organization's basic function in society in terms of the products and services it offers its clients. It explains why the organization exists and is usually emphasized in the mission statement. It should link to and inform the marketing plan, and in turn the plan must contribute towards the attainment of the firm's mission. The importance of the mission statement is explained as follows:

- Customers want to know what the organization stands for
- It is an important communication tool, both internally and externally
- It can be motivational for employees
- It is important for strategic management in ensuring that any plans are aligned to the mission of the business

The mission statement should outline:

- **Purpose** – why the organization exists
- **Strategy** – how it intends to compete, grow and achieve its stated objectives
- **Values** – its principles of business–social policy, and a commitment to staff and customers
- **Policies** and **standards** – in terms of behaviour and standards of service performance

A good mission statement should:

- Offer credibility to stakeholders
- Be unique to the organization in question
- Embrace specific capabilities of the organization
- Be aspirational to individuals

The vision defines where the organization wants to be in the future, and represents the positive and optimistic view of the organization's progression and development. The marketing plan should therefore support and complement the business' mission and vision.

A = Analysis of the Marketing Environment

This involves a thorough study of the broader trends within the economy and society, and a comprehensive analysis of markets, competitors and the company itself. There are a number of analytical techniques that can be used to analyse the business's internal environment. These have been explained earlier:

- SWOT Analysis
- McKinsey's 7S
- Porter's 5 Forces
- PESTLE Analysis

O = Objectives Setting

Objectives are what the organization wants to achieve in its operational activities. Objectives can be set at three different levels of the organization. These include corporate, business and functional (including marketing, finance, human resource and operations) which are outlined as follows:

Corporate objectives define specific goals for the organization as a whole. This may be expressed in concrete terms such as profitability, return on investment, growth of asset base and earnings per share. These will permeate the planning process and be reflected in the objectives for business units and functional objectives.

Business objectives define the goals of the various SBU or individual business units that form the corporation. For this reason, they are often used by multi-product or multi-service organizations like Virgin and Unilever, to help identify and differentiate the individual products and services.

Marketing objectives relate to what the organization wants to achieve in its marketing activities. Examples of marketing objectives include expansion of market share for a particular product, an increase in its customer base or growth in the usage of certain facilities.

Criteria for setting objectives

The **SMART criterion** should serve as a guide when objectives are set. This criterion stipulates that objectives should be:

S = Specific (objectives should be easily understood and clearly spelled out)

M = Measurable (objectives should be quantifiable with numbers)

A = Attainable (the set objectives should be achievable)

R = Relevant or Realistic (the firm should have the necessary resources to achieve its stated objectives)

T = Time-bound (objectives should be achieved within specified periods)

S = Strategy Development

Following the analysis of the marketing environment and the setting of marketing objectives, strategies are developed to explain and determine how the set objectives will be achieved. Strategies are the means of achieving the organization's stated objectives. Strategies can be set at several levels in any organization, ranging from the overall business (or group of businesses) through to the individuals who are working in it. More specifically, strategies can be set at corporate, business and functional levels of the company and these are explained as follows:

1) *Corporate Strategy* is concerned with the overall purpose and scope of the business to meet stakeholder expectations. This is a crucial level since it is heavily influenced by investors in the business and acts to guide strategic decision-making throughout the business. Corporate strategy is often stated explicitly in a 'mission statement'.

2) *Business Unit Strategy* is concerned more with how a business competes successfully in a particular market. It concerns strategic decisions about choice of products, meeting the needs of customers, gaining advantage over competitors, and exploiting or creating new opportunities etc.

3) *Operational Strategy* is concerned with how each part of the business is organized in order to deliver the corporate and business-unit level strategic direction. Operational strategy therefore focuses on issues of resources, processes, people etc.

There are a number of strategies that can be adopted to help in both growing the business and gaining competitive advantage respectively.

- The Ansoff's Matrix – growth strategies to help the firm achieve growth objectives, such as an increase in sales
- Porter's Generic Strategies – competitive strategies that will help the firm better compete in the marketplace and achieve specific objectives such as gaining market share.

The Ansoff's Matrix – Growth Strategies

The matrix was developed by applied mathematician and business manager Igor Ansoff, and was first published in *Harvard Business Review* in 1957. The Ansoff Matrix has helped many marketers and managers better understand the risks inherent in growing their business. It is also referred to as the **Product–Market Extension Grid** and is perhaps the most popular method employed by organizations in any attempt to grow their businesses. The strategy is based mainly on the manipulation of the two variables of markets and products to grow the business and subsequently help the firm achieve its objectives. This produces four possible strategy options, as shown in the diagram below.

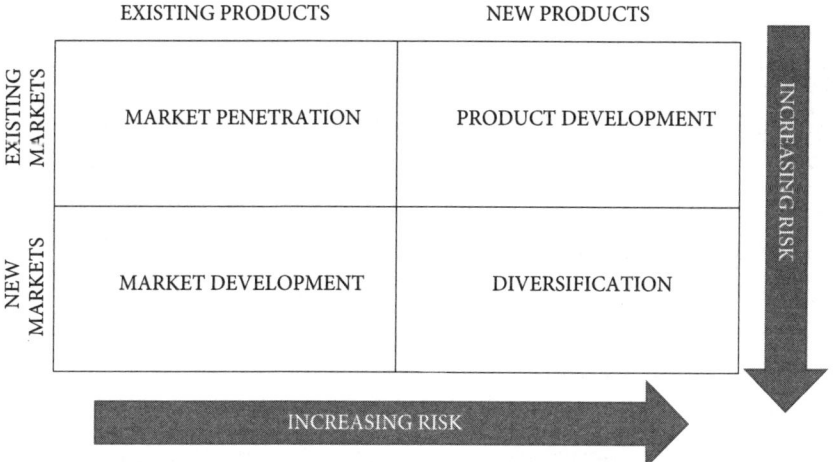

Figure 21: Ansoff's Matrix (1957)

Market Penetration

This involves selling **more** of the firm's existing products to its existing markets. Market penetration seeks to achieve four main objectives:

1) Maintain or increase the market share of current products – this can be achieved by a combination of competitive pricing strategies, advertising, sales promotion and perhaps more resources dedicated to personal selling.
2) Secure dominance of growth markets.
3) Restructuring a mature market by driving out competitors; this would require a much more aggressive promotional campaign, supported by a pricing strategy designed to make the market unattractive for competitors.
4) Increase usage by existing customers.

The market penetration strategy can be executed in a number of ways.

- Decreasing prices to attract new customers
- Increasing promotion and distribution efforts
- Acquiring a competitor in the same marketplace

Product Development

This approach requires the organization to develop modified products, which can appeal to existing markets. By tailoring the products specifically to the needs of existing customers, the organization can strengthen its competitive advantage. Apple is a strong proponent of this strategy, as seen by the continuous relaunching and upgrade of its iPhone products, targeted mainly at existing customers who want to upgrade to the latest versions of the phone.

The move typically involves extensive research, development and expansion of the company's product range. The product development strategy is employed when firms have a strong understanding of their current market and are able to provide innovative solutions to meet the needs of the existing market.

This strategy may be implemented in a number of ways:

1) Investing in research and development to create new products that cater to the existing market
2) Acquiring a competitor's product and merging resources to create a new product that better meets the need of the existing market
3) Forming strategic partnerships with other firms to gain access to each partner's distribution channels or brand

Market Development

This strategy involves expanding into new markets with existing products. The market development strategy is most successful if:

1) The firm owns proprietary technology that it can leverage into new markets;
2) Potential consumers in the new market are profitable (i.e., they possess disposable income);
3) Consumer behaviour in the new markets does not deviate too far from that of consumers in the existing markets.

The strategy may be achieved by way of expanding into any or a combination of the following:

- New markets geographically (e.g. international markets)
- New market segments
- New users for products.

Diversification

This implies developing new products for new markets. It is very expensive and risky because the organization might be entering into new areas in which it has no expertise. The Virgin Group, for example, has been very successful in its diversification efforts, and its product ranges now include airlines, trains, telecoms, media and gyms. For a business to adopt a diversification strategy, therefore, it must have a clear idea about what it expects to gain from the strategy and an honest assessment of the risks. Diversification could be **related or unrelated**.

1) **Related diversification.** There are potential synergies to be realized between the existing business and the new product/market. For example, a leather shoe producer that starts a line of leather wallets or accessories is pursuing a related diversification strategy.

2) **Unrelated diversification.** There are no potential synergies to be realized between the existing business and the new product/market. For example, a leather shoe producer that starts manufacturing phones is pursuing an unrelated diversification strategy.

Competitive Strategies – Porter's Generic Competitive Strategies

Porter's Generic Competitive Strategies are used to assist firms in deciding their basis for competing in the industries in which they operate. Porter's generic strategies offer ways of gaining competitive advantage – in other words, developing the 'edge' that ensures you make the sale and take it away from your competitors.

Markets where business competes

		Broad	Narrow
Source of Competitive Advantage	Costs	Cost Leadership	Cost Focus
	Differentiation	Differentiation Leadership	Differentiation Focus

Figure 22: Porter's Generic Competitive Strategies

Porter called the generic strategies Cost Leadership (no frills), Differentiation (creating uniquely desirable products and services) and Focus (offering a specialized service in a niche market). He then subdivided the Focus strategy into two parts: Cost Focus and Differentiation Focus.

Cost Leadership

The Cost Leadership strategy, as the name implies, involves being the leader in terms of cost in the firm's industry or market. Simply being among the lowest-cost producers is not good enough, as the firm may be open to attack by other low-cost producers who may undercut prices and therefore block the firm's attempts to increase market share.

The Cost Leadership strategy can be achieved in one of two ways:

- Increasing profits by reducing costs, while charging industry-average prices.
- Increasing market share by charging lower prices, while still making a reasonable profit on each sale because of reduced costs.

To achieve a successful Cost Leadership strategy entails the firm having:

- access to the capital needed to invest in technology that will bring costs down;
- very efficient logistics;
- a low-cost base in terms of labour, materials, facilities and a way of sustainably cutting costs below those of other competitors.

The greatest risk in pursuing a Cost Leadership strategy is that these bases or sources of cost reduction are not unique to the firm, and that other competitors copy your cost reduction strategies. Hence, it is imperative that the firm continuously seek out ways of reducing its costs bases.

Differentiation Strategy

Differentiation involves making the firm's products or services unique, different from and more attractive than those of the firm's competitors. Bases for such competitive differentiation can be achieved by means of any of the following:

- Product features
- Product functionality
- Product durability
- Product/service support
- Brand image that your customers value

To make a success of a Differentiation strategy, organizations need:

- good research, development and innovation;
- the ability to deliver high-quality products or services;
- effective sales and marketing, so that the market understands the benefits offered by the differentiated offerings.

Focus Strategy

Companies that use Focus strategies will tend to concentrate on particular niche markets and, by understanding the dynamics of that market and the specific needs of customers within it, develop uniquely low-cost or well-specified products for the market. Because such firms serve customers in their market particularly well, they tend to build strong brand loyalty amongst their customers. This makes their particular market segment less attractive to competitors.

As with broad market strategies, it is still critical to determine whether the firm will pursue Cost Leadership or Differentiation once the firm has selected a Focus strategy as its main strategic approach. This implies that Focus is not normally enough on its own. However, whether the firm adopts Cost Focus or Differentiation

Focus, the key to making a success of a generic Focus strategy is to ensure that the firm is providing or adding something extra as a result of serving only that market niche. Focusing on only one market segment due to the size of the firm can be dangerous, as bigger firms with more resources can enter the market and outplay the firm.

Determining Strategic Choices

The most appropriate strategy to adopt is a critical decision, because this can have implications for whether the firm can realize its stated objectives. Determining the choices of such strategies can be achieved using the SFA criteria – Suitability, Feasibility and Acceptability.

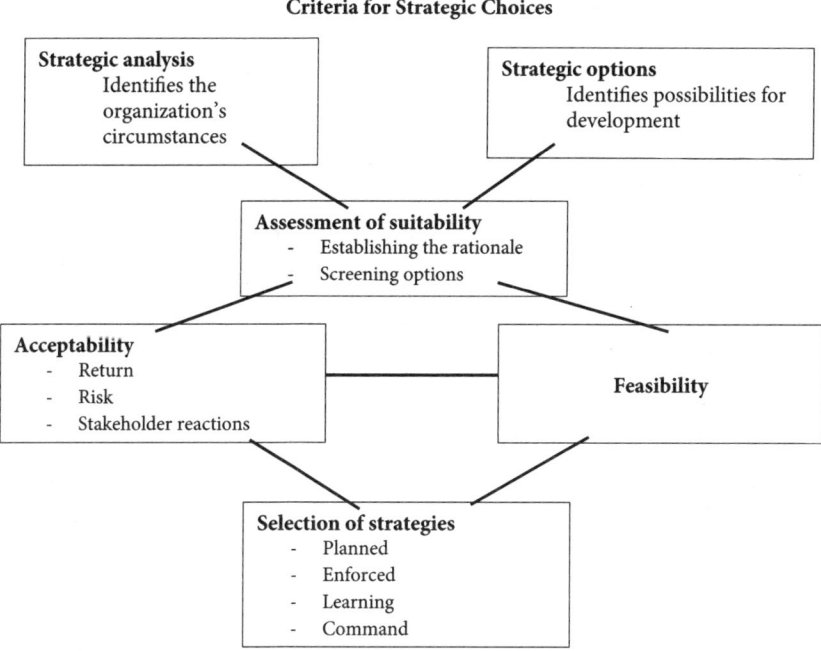

Figure 23: Criteria for Strategy Selection

Suitability

Suitability refers to the overall rationale of the strategy and its fit with the organization's mission. Suitability is a useful criterion for screening strategies, asking the following questions about strategic options:

- Does the strategy exploit the company strengths?
- How far does the strategy overcome the difficulties identified in the analysis?
- Does the option fit in with the organization's purposes?

Feasibility

Feasibility is concerned with the resources required to implement the chosen strategy. Resource issues to consider include the following:

1) Money/funding
2) People
3) Time
4) Information

Acceptability

Acceptability is concerned with the expectations of the identified stakeholders (mainly shareholders, employees and customers) with the expected performance outcomes. Acceptance of chosen strategies by stakeholders is dependent on a consideration for the levels associated with the 3Rs – namely **return, risk** and **reactions** of stakeholders.

- **Return** deals with the benefits expected by the stakeholders (financial and non-financial). For example, shareholders expect the increase of their wealth, employees expect an improvement in their careers and customers expect better value for money.
- **Risk** deals with the probability and consequences of failure of a strategy (financial and non-financial).
- **Reactions of stakeholders** anticipates the likely reaction of stakeholders.

T = Tactics

Tactics are measures or techniques that aid the achievement of strategies. Tactics in marketing usually include the use and manipulation of the 7Ps – examining how each of the following can be used to help in the attainment of the planned marketing objectives:

- Product
- Price
- Place
- Promotion
- People
- Process
- Physical Evidence

I = Implementation

Once marketing strategies and tactics have been set, it becomes necessary to turn them into action plans. Implementation of marketing plans includes the following three activities:

1) **Allocating tasks and responsibilities**: planning responsibilities and targets for teams and their individual members.
2) **Scheduling of marketing activities**: this is often helped by having a diagrammatic illustration of the marketing activities that will be carried out and the timetable by which they will be executed.
3) **Setting the marketing budget**: a financial statement showing how much the company intends to spend on its marketing activities in any given period.

C = Control

Once the marketing plan starts to be implemented, the task of management is to monitor and control what goes on. **Monitoring** means checking that everything is going according to plan. **Control** means taking corrective actions as early as possible if things are not going according to plan.

Regardless of the type or levels of control systems an organization needs, control may be depicted as a six-step feedback model:

1) **Determine what to control**. What are the objectives the organization hopes to accomplish?
2) **Set control standards**. What are the targets and tolerances?
3) **Measure performance**. What are the actual standards?
4) **Compare the performance to the standards**. How well does the actual match the plan?
5) **Determine the reasons for the deviations**. Are the deviations due to internal shortcomings or due to external changes beyond the control of the organization?
6) **Take corrective action**. Are corrections needed in internal activities to correct organizational shortcomings, or are changes needed in objectives due to external events?

The most effective control method to be adopted by the firm very much depends on the objectives set. Control methods include the following:

Benchmarking

Benchmarking is the process of comparing a company's performance to the performance of other companies. Management can do this by comparing business groups within a company, by comparing companies within an industry or by comparing companies across different industries. The idea behind benchmarking best practices is to identify the company's strengths and weaknesses, to make comparisons of functional activities and areas between the company and its specific competitors who are considered to be the best in those activities or areas. It is then possible to determine ways to emphasize the strengths and improve upon the weaknesses of the company, based on the findings of the analysis.

Benchmark tests can be conducted in terms of the following:

- Product quality or features
- The quality of services provided
- The efficiency of operational processes
- Financial and operational performance measures
- Competitor performances relative to the firm

Balanced scorecard method

The balanced scorecard is a management system control technique developed by Norton and Kaplan (1996) and it provides a useful link between setting objectives and measuring performance. Kaplan and Norton suggested that a balanced set of objectives should be developed and, at the same time, a complementary set of performance measures be set alongside them. The scorecard enables companies to monitor and measure the success of their strategies to determine how well they have performed.

As a result, a set of measures gives top managers a quick but comprehensive overview of the business, which can be an important tool for guiding performance and identifying key measurements in four categories or business perspectives:

1) **Financial Perspective** – Under the financial perspective, the goal of a company is to ensure that it earns a return on the investments made and manages key risks involved in running the business. The goals can be achieved by satisfying the needs of all players involved with the business, such as the shareholders, customers and suppliers. Since they are the providers of capital, the shareholders are an integral part of the business; they should be happy when the

company achieves financial success. They want to be sure that the company is continually generating revenues and that the organization meets key goals and targets such as improving profitability and developing new revenue sources. Steps taken to achieve such goals may include introducing new products and services, improving the company's value proposition and cutting down on the costs of doing business.

2) **Customer Perspective** – The customer perspective monitors how the firm is providing value to its customers and determines the level of customer satisfaction with the company's products or services. Customer satisfaction has long been a key indicator of the company's success, and how well a company treats its customers can obviously affect its profitability. The balanced scorecard considers the company's reputation versus the reputations of its competitors. Do customers have starkly differing views of the company and its main competitors? Such analysis enables the organization to step out of its comfort zone in order to view itself from the customer's point of view rather than just from an internal perspective.

Some of the strategies on which a company can focus in order to improve its reputation among customers include improving product quality, enhancing the customer shopping experience, delivering outstanding aftersales service, and adjusting the prices of its main products and services.

3) **Internal Business Processes Perspective** – A business's internal processes determine how well the entity runs as a whole. A balanced scorecard puts into perspective the measures and objectives that can help the business run more effectively. In addition, the scorecard helps evaluate the company's products or services and determine whether they conform to the standards that customers' desire. A key part of this perspective is aiming to answer the question: 'What is the firm good at?'.

The answer to that question can help the company formulate marketing strategies and pursue innovations that lead to the creation of new and improved ways of meeting the needs of customers.

4) **Learning and Growth Perspective** – Organizational capacity is important in optimizing goals and objectives with favourable results. The personnel in the organization's departments are required to demonstrate high performance in terms of leadership, the entity's culture, application of knowledge and skill sets. Proper infrastructure is required for the organization to deliver according to the expectations of management. For example, the organization should use the latest technology to automate activities and ensure a smooth flow of activities.

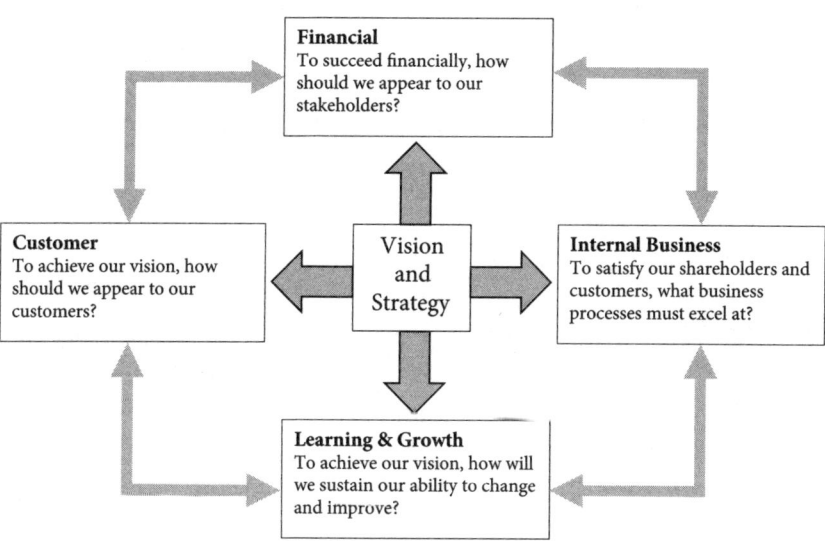

Figure 24: Balanced Scorecard Framework by Kaplan and Norton (1996)

The image below shows the high-level value-creation story through perspectives for mission-driven organizations.

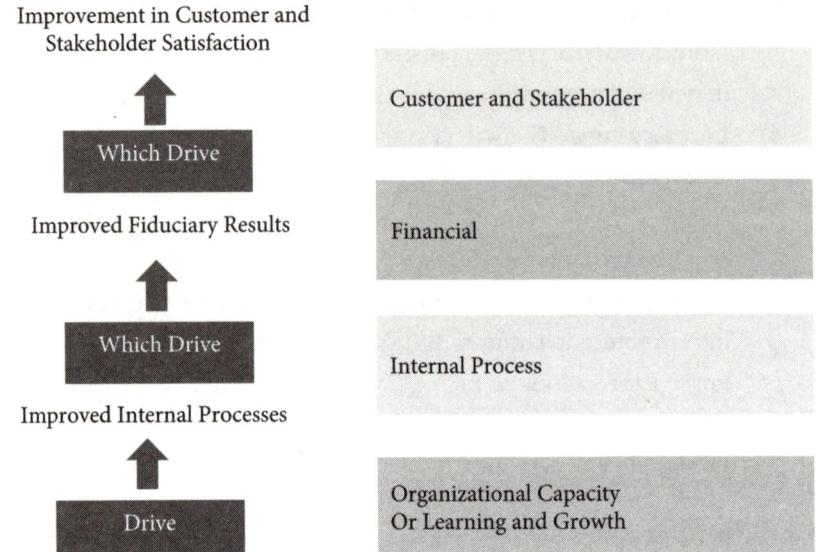

Figure 25: Outcomes of Balanced Scorecard Framework (Kaplan and Norton, 1996)

The Marketing Audit

The marketing audit is a comprehensive review of the marketing plan, including the business objectives and current activities, to determine if there are any areas for improvement. It looks into all aspects of the firm's marketing operations, its checklist examines:

- Marketing environment
- Marketing objectives
- Marketing strategies and tactics
- Implementation of marketing planning activities

When conducting a thorough marketing audit, marketing managers will be able to identify the plans weaknesses and strengths, so that managers will know where to place the firm's resources appropriately.

Conducting the marketing audit can enable managers to ask and review answers to the following questions.

- How is the business performing in terms of profitability and customer perception?
- What are your current marketing strategies? How have they evolved in the past year?
- Where is the business going? Can you reach that point with your current strategies?

CHAPTER FIFTEEN

International Marketing

As mentioned in the preceding chapter on marketing planning and strategy, the Ansoff's matrix proposed that firms can adopt a market development strategy whereby it sells its existing products in new markets. Such new markets include international markets. Additionally, the same model also proposed a diversification strategy, whereby the firm can develop new products and sell to new (international) markets.

In essence, the practice of marketing is not just confined to the company's domestic market but can also be extended into international markets. More than ever before, firms are today increasing the spread of their operations by expanding into international markets. The phrase 'the world is your market' is indeed being exploited by firms from all parts of the globe. Even mighty brands such as Apple generate over half of their revenues from outside its home market, the United States. There are many reasons why firms are entering international markets:

- These include the **saturation of the domestic market**, which leads firms either to seek other less competitive markets overseas
- **Diversifying risks and the emergence of new markets** – not over-relying on one single market coupled with the identification of new growth markets that provide distinct opportunities for the firm
- **To grow more sales and generate more profits** – Apple generates more than half of its sales from overseas markets

- **The stage in the product life cycle** – typically in the decline stage of the product life cycle, the firm will want to extend the product's lifespan by entering into foreign markets.
- **Increasing globalization of markets**, characterized by similar or homogeneous consumer behaviours, has made it possible by means of advances in technologies
- **Gaining competitive advantage** – the intensity of local competition in the firm's home market might compel it to enter foreign markets to gain an advantage over rivals.
- **Selling excess stock or capacity** – in situations where the firm cannot sell all of its stock in its home market, it may be necessary to enter new markets to dispose of such excess stock.
- **Government incentives** – These can include both the incentives offered by local governments as well as foreign governments. For example, the local government may offer incentives to locally based firms with the objectives of boosting exports to international markets. Foreign governments may also offer tax incentives to international firms with the aim of establishing manufacturing plants in their countries in order to create jobs.

Approaches To International Marketing

Companies can adopt different approaches in their efforts to become international market players. In developing 'global marketing strategy', it is useful to distinguish between **three forms of international expansion** that arise from a company's resources, capabilities and current international position.

1) **International marketing strategy** – the organization's objectives may relate primarily to the home market. However, some objectives will need to pay attention to overseas activity and therefore an international strategy is often required. Importantly, the competitive

advantage – important in strategy development – is usually developed mainly for the *home* market.

2) If the company is still mainly focused on its home markets, its strategies outside its home markets can be seen as international. For example, a dairy company might sell some of its excess milk and cheese supplies outside its home country. However, its main strategic focus is still directed to the home market.

3) **Multinational marketing strategy** – the organization is involved in a number of markets beyond its home country. However, it needs distinctive strategies for each of these markets because customer demand and, perhaps competition, will be different in each country. Importantly, competitive advantage is determined *separately for each country*.

4) **Global marketing strategy** – the organization treats the world as largely one market and one source of supply with little local variation. Importantly, competitive advantage is developed largely on a global basis. Companies talk about 'going global' when what they really mean is that they are moving internationally, outside their home countries. It is important to clarify precisely what such wording means because the strategic implications are completely different.

5) The business resources needed to sell internationally might typically include a sales team, brochures of products in various languages, and an office team to handle sales orders which is based in the home country. The business resources in going global are much greater. Typically, companies might need manufacturing plants in various lower-cost countries, global branding and advertising, sales teams in every major country, and expensive patent and intellectual property registration in many countries.

6) Hence, many companies do not have a 'global strategy' in the way that it is defined in international business literature. Even some major multinationals do not have a true global strategy, in the sense that their production is not completely integrated and they lack localized brands.

Process of Developing an International Marketing Strategy

Firms wanting to enter international markets should adopt and apply the appropriate steps to assist in this process. These steps or process includes the following;

1) Analysing the foreign market that the firm wants to enter
2) Identifying the company's competitive and other resources
3) Setting of international marketing objectives
4) Choosing the foreign market and entry method
5) Managing the marketing efforts in the foreign market

Analysing the International Market

In practice, there are **five main areas** to consider when analysing international opportunities:

1) **Customer demand in the main broad geographical areas:** market size, growth and history – including special customers such as large multinationals already involved as customers in a particular region.

2) **Competitors:** analysis of local and international companies already in country markets, their market shares and basic facilities – what major competitive advantages do they have?

3) **International and regional infrastructures:** what are the major costs involved in communicating, transporting and distributing in various parts of the world?

4) **Country politics and economic trends:** only some basic considerations may be required at this stage, such as political risk and economic growth – there may be too much to analyse in depth at such an early stage.

5) **International trade barriers, tariffs and quotas:** are there any major issues here that will support or restrict the market opportunity?

The PESTLE analysis framework explained in Chapter 3 (The Marketing Environment) can also be applied to analysing and better understanding the foreign market environment.

Once adequate research has been done to gather answers to the questions and areas identified above in analysing the foreign market, then the next stage in developing an international marketing strategy involves analysing the firm's competitive and other resources so as to exploit its resources to take advantage of the opportunities presented in the foreign market.

Identifying the company's own and other competitive resources

There are two main aspects to identifying the company's resources for international and global expansion:

- The reasons why the company wants to go international or global
- Sustainable competitive advantages of the company in its home market prior to going global. These will form the bedrock of how the company will go international or global.

Sustainable Competitive Advantage

These are the advantages that the firm enjoys over its competitors that cannot be easily imitated by others. They form the bedrock in strategy theory for the development of effective strategy. Unfortunately, they are easy to discuss in principle and more difficult to identify in practice.

Essentially, the argument is that the competitive advantages possessed by the company in its home market should form the basis of its international expansion strategy. For companies already in international markets, they will wish to focus on those advantages that allow them to outperform their rivals.

Analysing and Developing Sustainable Competitive Advantage

In order to identify the firm's basis for competitive advantage, it is imperative to conduct an internal analysis of its environment in order to specify and develop its:

- resources
- capabilities
- core competencies.

Resource-based View of Strategy

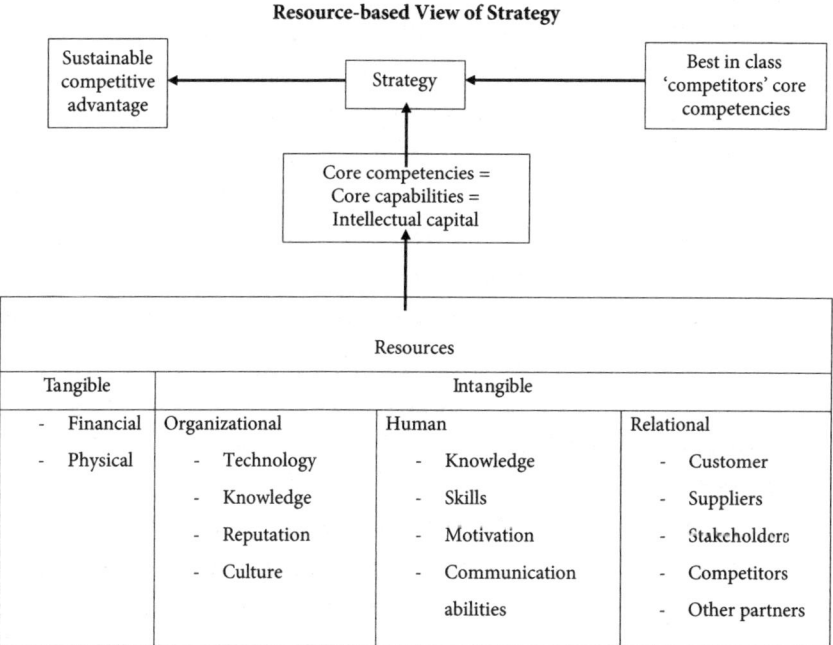

Figure 26: Resource-based View of Strategy Model

The resource-based view (RBV) strategy argues that organizations should look for sources of competitive advantage inside the company rather than within the competitive environment. In essence, the RBV model proposes that the firm should rely and exploit its resources to determine its core competencies and capabilities and as a result use these to gain competitive advantage over its rivals.

According to RBV proponents, it is much more feasible to exploit external opportunities using existing resources in a new way rather than trying to acquire new skills for each different opportunity. In the RBV model, resources are given the major role in helping companies to achieve higher organizational performance. There are two types of resources: tangible and intangible.

1) **Tangible assets** are physical things – land, buildings, machinery, equipment and capital. Physical resources can easily be bought in the market so they confer little advantage to the companies in the end because rivals can soon acquire the identical assets.

2) **Intangible assets** are those things that have no physical presence but can still be owned by the company – brand reputation, trademarks, intellectual property are all intangible assets. Unlike physical resources, brand reputation is built over a long time and is something that other companies cannot buy from the market. Intangible resources usually stay within a company and are the main source of sustainable competitive advantage.

The two critical assumptions of RBV are that resources must also be heterogeneous and immobile.

Heterogeneous. The first assumption is that skills, capabilities and other resources differ from one company to another. If organizations had the same amount and mix of resources, they could not employ different strategies to outcompete each other. What one company did, the other could simply follow, and no competitive advantage could be achieved. This is the scenario of perfect competition, yet real world markets are far from perfectly competitive and some companies, which are exposed to the same external and competitive forces (i.e. the same external conditions), are able to implement different strategies and outperform each other. Therefore, RBV assumes that companies achieve competitive advantage by using their different bundles of resources.

The competition between Apple Inc. and Samsung Electronics is a good example of how two companies that operate in the same industry – and which are therefore exposed to the same external forces – can achieve different organizational performance due to the difference in resources. Apple competes with Samsung in tablets and smartphone markets where Apple sells its products at much higher prices and, as a result, reaps higher profit margins. Why does Samsung not follow the same strategy? Simply because Samsung does not have the same brand reputation nor is it capable of designing user-friendly products in the same way as Apple.

Immobile. The second assumption of RBV is that resources are not mobile and do not move from company to company, at least in the short run. This immobility means that companies cannot replicate rivals' resources and implement similar strategies. Intangible resources, such as brand equity, processes, knowledge or intellectual property, are usually immobile.

Discovering Core Competencies

Core competencies are the defining capabilities or advantages that a business may have which distinguish it from the competition. Core competence is the foundation for sharpening a company's competitive edge, and it guides brand reputation, business growth and marketing strategy.

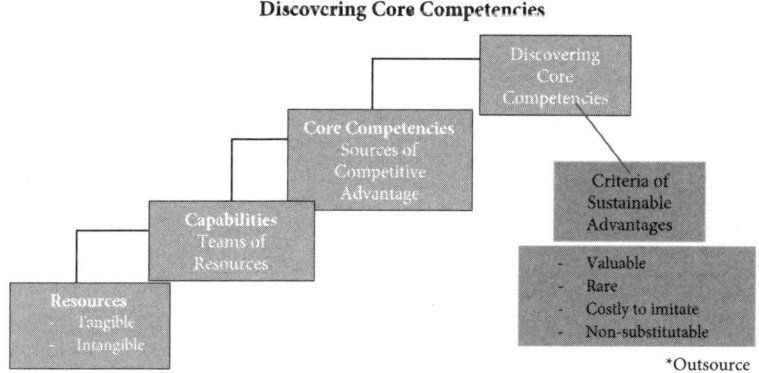

Figure 27: Discovering Core Competencies

To discover and specify the firm's core competencies, the firm should start by reviewing and analysing its resources. Such resources will help in determining its core competencies or strengths, which will serve as the basis for its competitive advantage.

Competitive advantage refers to the factors that gives the firm a distinct advantage over its rivals or competitors, without which the firm cannot differentiate itself from others. Such competitive advantage must be sustainable over the long term, which can be very difficult in practice. Hence, it is critical for the firm to continuously review and determine its basis for competitive advantage against the VRIO criteria:

- **V = Valuable.** This asks if a resource adds value by enabling a firm to exploit opportunities or defend against threats. If the answer is yes, then a resource is considered valuable. Resources are also valuable if they help organizations to increase the perceived customer value. This is done by increasing differentiation and/or decreasing the price of the product. The resources that cannot meet this condition lead to competitive disadvantage. It is important to continually review the value of the resources because constantly changing internal or external conditions can make them less valuable or useless.
- **R = Rare.** Resources that can only be acquired by one or very few companies are considered rare. Rare and valuable resources grant temporary competitive advantage. On the other hand, a situation where more than a few companies have the same resource or use the capability in a similar way, leads to competitive parity. This is because firms can use identical resources to implement the same strategies and no organization can achieve superior performance. Even though competitive parity is not the desired position, a firm should not neglect those resources that are valuable but common. Losing valuable resources and capabilities will hurt an organization because they are essential for staying in the market.
- **I = Imitable.** A resource is costly to imitate if other organizations cannot imitate, buy or substitute it at a reasonable price. Imitation can occur in

two ways: by directly imitating (duplicating) the resource or providing the comparable product/service (substituting). A firm that has valuable, rare and costly to imitate resources can achieve sustained competitive advantage (though this is not guaranteed). Barney (2002) has identified three reasons why resources can be hard to imitate:

- ✓ *Historical conditions.* Resources that were developed due to historical events or over a long period usually are costly to imitate.
- ✓ *Causal ambiguity.* Companies cannot identify the particular resources that are the cause of competitive advantage.
- ✓ *Social Complexity.* The resources and capabilities that are based on company's culture or interpersonal relationships.

- **O = Organization.** The resources itself do not confer any advantage for a company if it is not organized to capture the value from them. A firm must organize its management systems, processes, policies, organizational structure and culture to be able to fully realize the potential of its valuable, rare and costly-to-imitate resources and capabilities. Only then can the companies hope to achieve sustained competitive advantage.

Once the firm has analysed the foreign market and its internal capabilities, it should set the objectives to be achieved in the foreign market.

Setting International Marketing Objectives

With regard to international expansion, the company's objectives involve three important questions:

1) **Why go international?** The answer will determine the strategic approach.
2) **What profits** do we expect over what timescale and with what risk?
3) **What commitment** is needed and will be given by the top management team?

Examples of possible marketing objectives to be attained include:

- ✓ Gaining market share in the foreign market
- ✓ Generating sales and profits in the foreign market
- ✓ Launching new products in international markets
- ✓ Creating brand awareness in foreign markets

Following the specification of the firm's foreign market objectives, the next step in the international marketing process is to consider, determine and choose the most appropriate entry strategy that the firm needs to adopt in entering the foreign market.

Choosing Foreign Markets to Enter and Methods of Entry

Firms can enter foreign market via different entry strategies. The strategy for international expansion depends on two main topics:

1) **Country (or region of world) selected**
2) **Method of entry**

Importantly, the process of resolving these issues is circular – i.e. the choice of one will influence the choice of the other. For example, it might be that the best *method of entering* a country might be to acquire a company. However, the acquisition may be expensive and risky and therefore it might be better to select another country.

The decision of how to enter a foreign market can have a significant impact on the result of the firms. Expansion into foreign markets can be achieved via the following entry strategies.

- Exporting
- Licensing/Franchising
- Joint venture
- Direct investment
- Mergers and acquisitions
- Strategic alliances
- New, wholly owned overseas operations

Direct Exporting

Exporting is the marketing and direct sale of domestically produced goods in another country. Exporting is a traditional and well-established method of reaching foreign markets. Since exporting does not require that the goods be produced in the target country, no investment in foreign production facilities is required. Most of the costs associated with exporting take the form of marketing expenses.

Exporting commonly requires coordination among four players:

- exporter – a local person or firm sending products to the overseas importers
- importer – the local person or firm ordering the product from overseas exporters
- transport provider – in terms of shipping and delivery of exports
- government – in terms of providing export / import guidelines for companies engaging in this practice

Requirements for Export Marketing

- An understanding of the target market environment
- The use of market research and identification of market potential
- Decisions concerning product design, pricing, distribution and channels, advertising and communications

Government Incentives to Promote Exporting

It is becoming increasingly common for governments to promote exports to international markets and as such does provide a number of incentives to encourage local firms to boost exports. This is because exports increase jobs, bring in higher wages, and raise the standard of living for residents. As such, people become happier and more likely to support their national leaders.

Exports also increase the foreign exchange reserves held in the nation's central bank. Foreigners pay for exports either in their own currency or the US dollar. A country with large reserves can use it to manage their own currency's value. They have enough foreign currency to flood the market with their own currency. That lowers the cost of their exports in other countries.

Countries also use currency reserves to manage liquidity. That means they can better control inflation, which is too much money chasing too few goods. To control inflation, they use the foreign currency to purchase their own currency. That decreases the money supply, making the local currency worth more. Such export promotion incentives can include the following:

- **Tax incentives** – tax exemption on profits made from exports, for example
- **Subsidies** – A subsidy takes the form of a payment, provided directly or indirectly, to the receiving individual or business entity. Subsidies are generally seen as a privileged type of financial aid, as they lessen an associated burden that was previously levied against the receiver, or promote a particular action by providing financial support.
- **Governmental assistance** – for example, government backed low interest (soft) loans and government-financed international advertising
- **Free trade zones** – Free zones generally fall into one of four categories: free trade zones, export processing zones, special economic zones or industrial zones. Free trade zones, typically located near seaports or airports, mainly offer exemptions from national import and export duties on goods that are re-exported. Local services gain, though there is little, if any, value added to the goods traded. Export processing zones go a step further by focusing on exports with a significant value added, rather than only on re-exports. Special economic zones apply a multisectoral development approach and focus on both domestic and foreign markets. They offer an array of incentives including infrastructure, tax and custom exemptions, and simpler administrative procedures. Industrial zones are targeted at specific economic activities, say media or textiles, with infrastructure adapted accordingly.

Government Actions that Discourage Imports and Market Access

Conversely, some governments discourage imports so as to protect local firms for example. These import controls can manifest in any of the following ways.

- Tariffs – A tariff is a specific type of tax that a governing body places on goods or services entering or leaving the country. In theory, when a government initiates a tariff programme, the additional costs saddled upon the affected items discourages imports, which in turn impacts the balance of trade
- Import controls – an action taken by a government to limit the number of goods that can be brought into a country from abroad to sell
- Non-tariff barriers – A non-tariff barrier is a trade restriction – such as a quota, embargo or sanction – that countries use to further their political and economic goals. Countries usually opt for non-tariff barriers (rather than traditional tariffs) in international trade.

Licensing

Licensing essentially permits a company in the target country to use the property of the licensor. Such property usually is intangible, such as trademarks, patents and production techniques. The licensee pays a fee in exchange for the rights to use the intangible property and possibly for technical assistance.

Because little investment is required on the part of the licensor, licensing has the potential to provide a very large ROI (return on investment). However, because the licensee produces and markets the product, potential returns from manufacturing and marketing activities may be lost.

A contractual agreement is required, whereby one company (the licensor) makes an asset available to another company (the licensee) in exchange for royalties, license fees or some other form of compensation. Suitable assets include:

- Patent
- Trade secret

- Brand name
- Product formulations

Special License Agreements

- **Contract Manufacturing.** Companies provide technical specifications to a subcontractor or local manufacturer. The subcontractor then oversees production. Such arrangements offer several advantages. The licensing firm can specialize in product design and marketing, while transferring responsibility for ownership of manufacturing facilities to contractors and subcontractors.
- **Franchising** is another variation of licensing strategy. A franchise is a contract between a parent company-franchiser and a franchisee that allows the franchisee to operate a business developed by the franchiser in return for a fee and adherence to franchise-wide policies and practices.

But a number of questions will need to be answered as part of the broader decision to consider franchising as a suitable and effective licensing option, including:

- Will local consumers buy your product?
- How tough is the local competition?
- Does the government respect trademark and franchiser rights?
- Can the profits be easily repatriated?
- Can you buy all the supplies you need locally?
- Is commercial space available and are rents affordable?
- Are your local partners financially sound and do they understand the basics of franchising?

Advantages of Licensing

- Provides additional profitability with little initial investment
- Provides method of circumventing tariffs, quotas and other export barriers
- Attractive ROI

- Low costs to implement
- License agreements should have cross-technology agreements to inequities

Disadvantages of Licensing

- Limited participation on the part of licensee
- Returns may be lost if the licensee underperforms
- Lack of control on the part of licensor
- Licensee may become competitor
- Licensee may exploit company resources

Joint Ventures

A joint venture (JV) is a business arrangement in which two or more parties agree to pool their resources for accomplishing a specific task, which can be a new project or any other business activity. In a JV, each of the participants is responsible for profits, losses and costs associated with it. However, the venture is its own entity, separate from the participants' other business interests.

There are three main reasons why companies form a JV:

- **Leverage resources**. A joint venture can take advantage of the combined resources of both companies to achieve the goal of the venture. One company might have a well-established manufacturing process, while the other company might have superior distribution channels.
- **Cost savings**. By using economies of scale, both companies in the JV can leverage their production at a lower per-unit cost than they would separately. This is particularly appropriate with technology advances that are costly to implement. Other cost savings because of a JV can include sharing advertising or labour costs.
- **Combined Expertise**. The companies or parties forming a joint venture might each have unique backgrounds, skillsets and expertise. When combined through a JV, each company can benefit from the other's expertise and talent within their company

A JV will typically be characterized by the following:

- Entry strategy for a single target country in which the partners share ownership of a newly created business entity
- Builds upon each partner's strengths

Advantages of Joint Ventures

- Allows for risk sharing – financial and political
- Provides opportunity to learn new environment
- Provides opportunity to achieve synergy by combining strengths of partners
- May be the only way to enter the market in the presence of barriers imposed by foreign governments

Limitations of Joint Ventures

- Requires more investment than a licensing agreement
- Must share rewards as well as risks
- Requires strong coordination among the partners
- Potential for conflict among partners
- Partner may become a competitor

Mergers and Acquisitions

A **merger** is a combination of two previously separate firms, which is achieved by forming a completely new business into which the two original firms are integrated. A merger can be seen as a decision made by two businesses that are broadly equal in terms of factors such as size, scale of operations or customers.

An acquisition is when one company purchases most or all of another company's shares to gain control of that company. Purchasing more than 50 per cent of a target firm's stock and other assets allows the acquirer to make decisions about the newly acquired assets without the approval of the company's shareholders. Acquisitions, which are very common in business, may occur with the target company's approval (friendly takeover), or in spite of its disapproval (hostile takeover). Examples of high-profile acquisitions include:

- Microsoft's acquisition of LinkedIn
- Facebook's acquisition of WhatsApp

If a company wants to expand its operations to another country, buying an existing company in that country could be the easiest way to enter a foreign market. The purchased business will already have its own personnel, a brand name and other intangible assets, which could help to ensure that the acquiring company will start in a new market with a solid base.

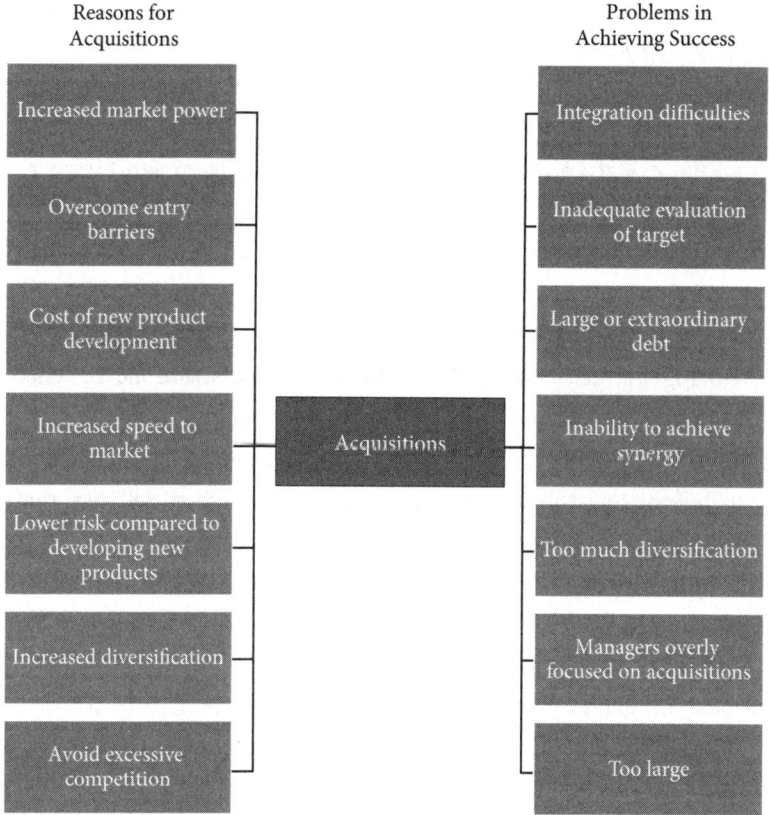

Figure 28: Reasons for and challenges associated with acquisitions

Strategic Alliances / Global Strategic Partnerships / Strategic International Alliances

Another way to enter a new market is through a strategic alliance with a local partner. A strategic alliance involves a contractual agreement between two or more enterprises stipulating that the involved parties will cooperate in a certain way for a certain time to achieve a common purpose. To determine if the alliance approach is suitable for the firm, the firm must decide what value the partner could bring to the venture in terms of both tangible and intangible aspects. The advantages of collaborating with a local firm are that the local firm likely understands the local culture, market and ways of doing business better than an outside firm. Partners are especially valuable if they have a recognized, reputable brand name in the country or have existing relationships with customers that the firm might want to access.

The best strategic alliances are ones that offer clear benefits to the audiences of both brands. When the strategic partnership appeals to both audiences, then the two businesses are able to expand their reach and generate more sales. It's a win-win strategy!

Examples of successful strategic alliances include the following:

- **T-Mobile and Taco Bell**

  During the 2019 Super Bowl, Taco Bell and T-Mobile unveiled an attractive brand partnership: T-Mobile customers could claim a free Taco Bell taco every Tuesday through the T-Mobile app, just for being a T-Mobile customer – no purchase needed at Taco Bell. Yes, that's it: All customers needed to do to get a free taco was to stick with their T-Mobile plan, encouraging brand loyalty to T-Mobile. Plus, since the promotion drew customers to Taco Bell regularly, it's likely that they bought other food or drinks there – and made going to Taco Bell a habit, even after the promotion ended.

  Another reason for the strategic alliance's success? As Convince and Convert explains, 'The [two brands'] customer bases are naturally aligned in that they skew male, they skew younger, and they skew toward value seekers.' That, coupled with the investment in Super Bowl ads and social media campaigns, made it a partnership worth talking about.

- **Louis Vuitton and BMW**

  Although they might seem very different, Louis Vuitton and BMW are both exclusive luxury brands that focus on craftsmanship. Plus, those who can afford a BMW vehicle probably can also afford a Louis Vuitton bag. Because of their shared audience, goals and values, the two brands partnered up to create a collection of Louis Vuitton bags, custom made to pair with the BMW i8 sports car. According to Patrick-Louis Vuitton, Head of Special Orders at Louis Vuitton, 'This collaboration with BMW epitomizes our shared values and creativity, technological innovation and style.'

  The bags' sleek black outer colour and electric blue lining match the car's design perfectly, and they're made of an innovative, unlikely material – carbon fibre, just like the i8's passenger cell. Plus, the four-piece set of bags fits perfectly into the i8's parcel shelf. The set may have retailed for a whopping $20,000, but that might be seen as a reasonable price for someone who already had a car worth over $135,000.

- **Hewlett-Packard and Disney**

  This alliance formed back when Mr Hewlett, Mr Packard and Mr Disney were all still involved with their respective companies. During the creation of *Fantasia*, Disney purchased audio equipment from Hewlett-Packard. The strategic alliance continued onwards, as Disney relied heavily on HP's development and IT team for its own infrastructure. In fact, at current-day Disney attractions, the Imagineering team is still quite married to the HP systems architecture. During the design and build phase of Disney's Mission: SPACE, HP engineers and Disney imagineers were working side by side to create the most technologically advanced ride yet.

- **Starbucks and Barnes & Noble**

  Here is a matchup that has stood the test of time. Whereas many brick and mortar bookstores have folded due to lack of customer base, the few that have formed strategic alliances have continued to prosper. One example is Barnes & Noble, collaborating with Starbucks. Over the years, Starbucks has become synonymous with coffee; like it or hate it, you instantly recognize the name. With a Starbucks location in most (if not all) Barnes & Noble bookstores, customers have twice the reason to shop there. Coffee break and browse the latest bestsellers shelf all in one stop.

- **Target and Lilly Pulitzer**
  Lilly Pulitzer is a high-end women's fashion brand known for its signature colourful patterns. Due to its pricing, however, Lilly Pulitzer isn't accessible to most shoppers. Plus, the brand's own stores are largely based in the eastern and southern US, further limiting brand awareness and accessibility.

  In 2015, though, the brand first partnered with Target to release a more affordable, limited-edition Lilly Pulitzer collection in Target stores and on Target.com. This made the Lilly Pulitzer brand more affordable and accessible to shoppers across the country. The alliance also generated buzz for Target, since they were carrying quality brand name items from a sought-after designer.

  The collection didn't just generate buzz – the first release sold out within hours (and in some stores, within minutes). This prompted other Lilly Pulitzer and Target collaborations in the years to come, all of which have sold out quickly.

Strategic partnerships are defined by the following characteristics:

- Participants remain independent following formation of the alliance
- Participants share the benefits of alliance as well as control over the performance of assigned tasks
- Participants make ongoing contributions in technology, products and other key strategic areas
- Two or more companies develop a joint long-term strategy
- The relationship is reciprocal

- Partners' vision and efforts are global
- The relationship is organized along horizontal lines (not vertical)
- When competing in markets not covered by the alliance, participants retain national and ideological identities

The Nature of Global Strategic Partnerships

In a global strategic partnership, two or more firms from different countries work as a team. They pool their resources or skills to provide better products or services. Furthermore, they reach a broader audience through collaboration. Firms engage in global strategic partnerships because they believe the partnership will lead to synergy, which means increased economic benefits.

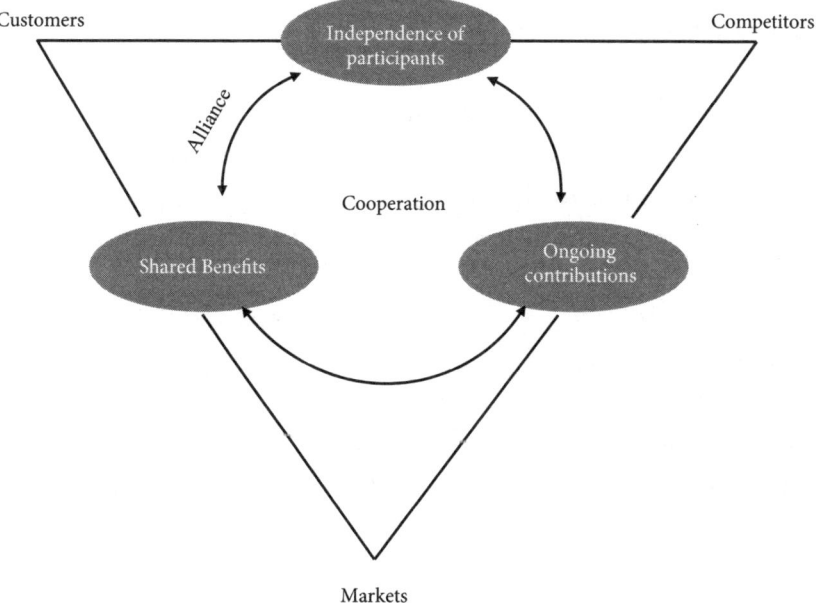

Figure 29: Nature of Global Strategic Alliances

Critical Success Factors in Alliances

- **Mission:** Successful GSPs create win-win situations, where participants pursue objectives based on mutual need or advantage.

- **Strategy**: A company may establish separate GSPs with different partners; strategy must be thought out up front to avoid conflicts.
- **Governance:** Discussion and consensus must be the norms. Partners must be viewed as equals.
- **Culture:** Personal chemistry is important, as is the successful development of a shared set of values.
- **Organization:** Innovative structures and designs may be needed to offset the complexity of multi-country management.
- **Management**: Potentially divisive issues must be identified in advance and clear, unitary lines of authority established that would result in commitment by all partners.

Problems Associated with Strategic Alliances

Four common problem areas:

1) Each partner has a different dream
2) Each must contribute to the alliance and each must depend on the other to a degree that justifies the alliance
3) Differences in management philosophy, expectations and approaches
4) No corporate memory

New, Wholly Owned Subsidiary

This involves the process of establishing of a new, wholly owned subsidiary (also called a greenfield venture). This is often complex and potentially costly, but it affords the firm maximum control and has the most potential to provide above-average returns. The costs and risks are high given the costs of establishing a new business operation in a new country. The firm may have to acquire the knowledge and expertise of the existing market by hiring host-country nationals – possibly either from competitive firms – or from costly consultants. An advantage is that the firm retains control of all its operations.

Because the parent company owns all the shares of a wholly owned subsidiary, there are no minority shareholders. The subsidiary operates with the permission of the parent company, which may or may not have a direct input into the subsidiary's operations and management. This may make it an unconsolidated subsidiary.

For example, a wholly owned subsidiary may be in a country different from that of the parent company. The subsidiary probably has its own senior management structure, product and clients. Having a wholly owned subsidiary may help the parent company maintain operations in diverse geographic areas and markets or separate industries. These factors help hedge against changes in the market or geopolitical and trade practices, as well as declines in industry sectors.

A popular example of a wholly owned subsidiary system is Volkswagen AG, which wholly owns Volkswagen Group of America, Inc. and its distinguished brands: Audi, Bentley, Bugatti, Lamborghini (wholly owned by Audi AG) and Volkswagen.

In addition, Marvel Entertainment and EDL Holding Company LLC are wholly owned subsidiaries of The Walt Disney Company. Coffee giant Starbucks Japan is a wholly owned subsidiary of Starbucks Corp.

Advantages and Disadvantages of a Wholly Owned Subsidiary

- Although a parent company has operational and strategic control over its wholly owned subsidiaries, the overall control is typically less for an acquired subsidiary with a strong operating history overseas. When a company hires its own staff to manage the subsidiary, forming common operating procedures is much less complicated than when taking over a company with established leadership.

- In addition, the parent company may apply its own data access and security directives for the subsidiary as a method of lessening the risk of losing intellectual property to other companies. Similarly, using similar financial systems, sharing administrative services and creating similar marketing programmes helps reduce costs for both companies, and a parent company directs how its wholly owned subsidiary's assets are invested.

- However, establishing a wholly owned subsidiary may result in the parent company paying too much for assets, especially if other companies are bidding on the same business. In addition, establishing relationships with vendors and local clients often takes time, which may hinder company operations; cultural differences may become an issue when hiring staff for an overseas subsidiary.
- The parent company also assumes all the risk of owning a subsidiary, and that risk may increase when local laws differ significantly from the laws in the parent company's country.

Mode	Conditions Favouring this Mode	Advantages	Disadvantages
Exporting	• Limited sales potential in target country: little product adaptation required • Distribution channels close to plants • High target country production costs • Liberal import policies • High political risk	• Minimizes risk and investment • Speed of entry • Maximizes scale • Uses existing facilities	• Trade barriers & tariffs add to costs • Transport costs • Limits access to local information • Company viewed as an outsider
Licensing	• Import and investment barriers • Legal protection possible in target environment • Low sales potential in target country • Large cultural distance • Licensee lacks ability to become a competitor	• Minimizes risk and investment • Speed of entry • Able to circumvent trade barriers • High ROI	• Lack of control over use of assets • Licensee may become competitor • Knowledge spillovers • License period is limited

Joint Venture	• Import barriers • Large cultural distance • Assets cannot be fairly priced • High sales potential • Some political risk • Government restrictions on foreign ownership • Local company can provide skills, resources, distribution networks, brand name, etc.	• Overcomes ownership restrictions and cultural distance • Combines resources of two companies • Potential for learning • Less investment required	• Difficult to manage • Dilution of control • Greater risk than exporting & licensing • Knowledge spillovers • Partner may become a competitor
Direct Investment	• Import barriers • Small cultural distance • Assets cannot be fairly priced • High sales potential • Low political risk	• Greater knowledge of local market • Can better apply specialized skills • Minimizes knowledge spillover • Can be viewed as an insider	• Higher risk than other modes • Requires more resources and commitment • May be difficult to manage the local resources

Figure 30: Comparisons of Foreign Market Expansion Strategies

Key Considerations in Choosing Foreign Entry Market Strategies

After assessing the environment in the selected country, how should the firm decide which are the most suitable countries to enter and which is the most appropriate entry strategy? The following factors should be considered:

- **Speed** – How quickly does the organization wish to enter your selected market?
- **Costs** – What is the cost of entering that market?
- **Flexibility** – How easy is it to enter/leave your chosen market?
- **Risk Factor** – What is the political risk of entering the market? What are the competitive risks? How competitive is the market?
- **Payback period** – When does the organization wish to obtain a return from entering the market? Are there pressures to break even and return a profit within a certain period?
- **Long-term objectives** – What does the organization wish to achieve in the long term by operating in the foreign market? Will it establish a presence in that market and then move onto others?

Managing Marketing Operations in International Markets

Once the firms has made the decision to enter a foreign market with any of the previously discussed entry strategies, then the decision has to be made as regards how it is going to manage its marketing operations in the foreign market. More specifically, firms operating in international markets have a number of choices pertaining to managing the attendant and supporting its marketing mix activities. The following three choices or approaches should be considered:

1) Standardization
2) Adaptation
3) Hybrid

The **Standardized marketing mix** involves selling the same products and using the same marketing approaches worldwide

The **Adapted marketing mix** involves adjusting the marketing mix elements in each target market, bearing more costs but hoping for a larger market share and ROI

The **Hybrid mix** implies using a combination of both standardization and adaptation approaches. Some aspects of the marketing mix may be the same such as the product but other aspects such as price may be different.

Standardization

The adoption and practice of standardization should be considered in the context of product, pricing and marketing communications, particularly advertising, branding and packaging. It may include the standardization of products across markets as well as standardization of the marketing mix worldwide.

Standardization is deemed appropriate under the following conditions:

- Commonalities in customers' needs across countries
- The 'made in' image is important to a product's perceived value – such as France for perfumes, Sheffield for stainless steel
- Homogeneity of markets – in other words markets available without adaptation, for products such as denim jeans
- Cultural insensitivity

Benefits of Standardization

- Economies of scale in production, marketing/communications, research and development
- Minimizes costs as standards are same everywhere
- Easier management and control of foreign market operations
- Addresses the needs of global consumers – homogeneous consumer groups sharing similar interests and product/brand preferences. Some products have no cultural sensitivity associated with them such as paper clips for example.
- Allows for global branding – using the same brand name, logo, image and positioning everywhere in the world

Adaptation

This involves the firm changing its marketing activities in terms of the marketing mix to reflect the needs of the local or foreign market served. The term **Glocal** (going global but staying local) is used to explain the concept of adaptation. Firms such as Starbucks and McDonald's are proponents of this approach.

Adaptation strategy implies changing various aspects of products and services to a considerable extent in order to meet the needs of consumers in international markets taking into account their differences. Adaptation strategy offers advantages of meeting differences of local markets at various levels, and in this way achieving greater levels of customer satisfaction. When pursuing product adaptation strategy differences of specific markets can be addressed at product development stage, accommodating differences in customer wants and needs in an effective manner.

There are different forms of adaptation, each for different reasons:

- **Mandatory Adaptation:** Adapting products to local requirements so that they can legally and physically operate in the respective countries – for example, driving on the left in the United Kingdom.
- **Local Non-Mandatory Adaptation:** Adapting a product to better meet the needs of the local market, or developing new brands for individual local markets, even though such adaptation is not required.
- **Modular Adaptation**: Offer parts (modules) that can be assembled worldwide in different configurations, depending on market needs. General Motors has established a modular product architecture for all its global automobile products. Future GM cars will be designed using a combination of components from 70 different body modules and about 100 major mechanical components (e.g. engines, power trains and suspension systems).

Core Product Strategy: Involves using a standardized strategy for the core product worldwide, but varying certain aspects of the offering (such as product ingredients or advertising) from market to market. There are three product strategies for firms to consider:

- **Straight product extension** means marketing a product in a foreign market without any change
- **Product adaptation** involves changing the product to meet local conditions or wants
- **Product invention** consists of creating something new for a specific country market
- Maintain or reintroduce earlier products
- Create new products

Adaptation is necessitated for the following reasons.

- Differences in cultures
- Differences in consumers income levels which can affect product design including the number of features and quality
- Differences in market structure in terms of competition and distribution systems for example
- Different climates and weather patterns as is the case in designing clothing for example
- Different legal systems, requirements and regulations
- Availability and level of local skills to support complex product design for example
- Differing product uses – bicycles may be the everyday transport in some parts of South East Asia as compared to its recreational use in the US for example

Hybrid: Compromise between standardization vs. adaptation argument can be achieved in a way that standardization can be applied in order to develop global marketing strategies in general, at the same time when applying adaptation to address unique aspects of local markets. In other words, standardization and adaptation strategies do not have to be mutually exclusive; however, an adequate level of balance needs to be maintained between the two. The case study of McDonald's can be mentioned to illustrate this point. McDonald's exercises standardization to a great extent in supply-chain management, employee relations, service processes and many other business processes, thus achieving economies of scale in several levels.

At the same time, the company uses adaptation through introducing Maharaja Mac in India, McArabia in Middle East, and McNuggets with chilli garlic sauce in China. Adaptation relates to McDonald's marketing strategy as well. For example, the fast-food chain has introduced Kaisu Burger in Singapore, after locally popular comic character Mr Kaisu. Thus, McDonald's is able to achieve advantages of both, standardization and adaptation strategies in global marketplace.

The notion of 'Think Global, Act Local' relates to this approach to a certain extent. Another effective illustration of this strategy can be observed in marketing of Unilever's 'Dove' brand of soaps. Scenery, text and other elements of 'Dove' television advertisement are the same for all markets, however, models featuring in advertisements and the language used by those models are adapted according to local culture for each individual market.

To summarize discussions, it is important for global businesses in the twenty-first century to be striving to take advantage of both strategies – standardization, as well as adaptation through maintaining an adequate balance between the two. In this way global businesses can take advantage of benefits offered by standardization such as achieving economies of scale and exercising the same competitive advantage for all markets, at the same time when taking advantage of benefits offered by adaptation as well such as addressing unique needs of local customers and responding to changes in local marketplace in rapid manner.

It is important to note that this essay has presented discussion of standardization vs. adaptation argument mainly with disregard to industry-specific factors, and in real-life business environment the extent of standardization or adaptation is different for each industry.

CASE STUDY

Revolut – Revolutionizing Mobile Banking

Like so many apps, Revolut was built with the intended purpose of fixing a personal issue. Nikolay Storonsky (co-founder and CEO) travelled a lot and was wasting hundreds of pounds on foreign transaction fees, which he understood as an employee at Credit Suisse to be ridiculously excessive.

After failing to find a bank that would cover multiple currencies, Storonsky and Vladyslav Yatsenko (co-founder and CTO) left their jobs at Credit Suisse to solve this issue. They started working on Revolut in Canary Wharf's Level39 tech incubator, a hub for fintech startups. Instead of working with the financial tech available, Revolut removed the middle-men and brought infrastructure in-house. Storonsky cites this as the route to financial stability, by reducing the amount of friction between Revolut and the user.

Revolut is a British financial technology company headquartered in London, England, that offers banking services. It was founded in 2015 by Nikolay Storonsky and Vlad Yatsenko.

On 26 April 2018, Revolut announced that it had raised a further $250 million in a funding round led by Hong Kong-based DST Global, reaching a total valuation of $1.8 billion and thus becoming a unicorn. DST Global was founded by Yuri Milner, who has been backed by the Kremlin in his previous investments.

Revolut's revolutionary app-based financial service provides all its services and transactions offered to customers via its app. It has 1.1 million daily active users as at December 2020 compared to 0.3 million in 2016. It generated revenues of £160 million as at December 2019 from £2.3 in 2016. The average daily customer sign up has grown from 3,250 in 2017 to 12,000 in 2019 and the customer contributions (amount of money Revolut makes from customer transactions) has risen from -£1.52 to £24 in 2019. The average customer deposit has grown from £251 in 2018 to £305 in 2019. Funding for the company has also increased steeply from £10 million in 2016 to £917 in 2019 (Business of Apps, 2020).

In December 2018, Revolut secured a Challenger bank licence from European Central Bank, facilitated by the Bank of Lithuania, authorizing it to accept deposits and offer consumer credits, but not to provide investment services. At the same time, an Electronic Money Institution licence was also issued by the Bank of Lithuania. In July 2019, Revolut launched commission-free stock trading in New York Stock Exchange and NASDAQ, initially for customers in its Metal plan. This was subsequently made available to all users. In October 2019, the company announced a global deal with Visa, following which it would expand into 24 new markets and hire around 3,500 additional staff.

In February 2020, Revolut completed a funding round that more than tripled its value, valuing the company at £4.2 billion and becoming the United Kingdom's most valuable financial technology startup. In August 2020, Revolut launched its financial app in Japan. In November 2020, Revolut became profitable and in January 2021, the company announced that it had applied for a UK banking license.

That desire to be more than a one-nation challenger bank may have provided Revolut with stronger footing on the funding side, as it was valued at $5.5 billion in 2019, higher than its three competitors N26, Monzo and Starling Bank. Revolut aims to use the $500 million it received in funding to acquire other tech companies, specifically focused on travel aggregation platforms. It also intends to launch more banking services in the United States.

Services Offered

Revolut earns most of its revenue through a process called interchange, in which it takes 0.2 per cent of each transaction fee. For the first few years, this did not translate to much, but as Revolut has added more users (12 million in 2020) the 0.2 per cent fees have started to add up. Alongside the small commission it take from debit cards, it also offers two premium tiers:

Premium: unlimited foreign exchange, double free ATM withdrawals abroad and travel insurance.

Metal: all premium features plus one per cent cashback with any currency (including crypto), quadruple free ATM withdrawals abroad, cashback and discounts.

Last year, Revolut launched a commission-free stocking trading app in the vein of Robinhood and a cryptocurrency trader. It also launched a Junior account, aimed at teaching 7 to 17 year olds about responsible spending and budgeting. Other mainstream financial services provided to its customers include the following.

Money Transfers

Revolut provides bank transfers to over 120 countries and customers can send money abroad up to ten times cheaper. Traditional banks and other banking services have markups on their exchange rate or hidden charges. However, with Revolut, customers can send money internationally for free in a total cost of sending £1,000. Money exchange with Revolut is fair and transparent. There are no fees needed in each transfer. Standard and premium accounts can send the money for free with an estimated arrival of up to two working days. However, if customers want to turbo-boost your money transfer, there is a small incurring fee. Moreover, customers can pay easily by setting up recurring payments for your on-the-go bills.

Vaults

Customers can reach their financial goals with Revolut in an easy and speedy manner. Customers can set up for their vaults in less than a minute and immediately start saving and can choose to round up each transaction, make a one-off contribution, or set up a recurring payment. Moreover, when customers make purchase with Revolut, they will automatically round up the transaction to the nearest whole number and they will place the difference into the customer's vault. This service is also applicable in cryptocurrencies.

Personal Loans

The company also offers short-term loans that can save customers an average of 50 per cent compared to banks. Customers can quickly check your personalized quote and instantly receive your money.

Cryptocurrency

Revolut claims to provide the easiest and fastest method to hold, exchange and buy Bitcoin, Bitcoin Cash, Ether, Litecoin and Ripple at the best possible rate. Additionally, the firm claims that there are no hidden extra charges associated with this service.

Mobile Phone Insurance

Revolut also offers customers mobile phone insurance services covering all types of accidental damages and malfunctions. For this service, the company charges £1 per week and customers can save 56 per cent as compared to other insurance providers.

Travel Insurance

The Pay-per-Day Travel Insurance of Revolut uses a geolocation technology. Thus, it only charges for the days when you are abroad. For as low as £1, customers can have dental and medical coverage.

Currency Converter

Revolut offers its customers the most common conversion rates instantly accessible via its app on their mobile devices.

Business Account

Revolut also provides corporate accounts including international payments for businesses. The account can receive, exchange and hold over 25 currencies without charge deductions. Even in international money transfers, there are no transfer fees. Moreover, business clients will receive a prepaid business card linked to the current account of their company. In this way, business clients can track the business expenses, set limits and easily block the card of the business's employees when lost.

Business clients can sync their transactions and receive real-time notifications into an accounting platform available in Revolut Connect. There is also an open API that allows business clients to automate cross-border business payments, send payouts and monitor transactions to the business's needs.

Revolut Expansion into International Markets

Unlike its major competitors Monzo and Starling, Revolut is far more Euro-centric. It works in all EU and European Economic Area countries. It also works with countries that have trade and data transfer agreements with the EU, such as Canada, Japan and Australia. It also recently launched in the United States. As at December 2020, Revolut is present in 37 countries.

In April 2019, Revolut announced plans to launch in as many as 24 new markets and hire 3,500 new staff, powered by a new partnership with payment services giant and card issuer Visa. The news came as Europe's biggest challenger banking service announced it will 'primarily' issue Visa-branded cards during the next stage of its global expansion.

Revolut also revealed that Australia, Brazil, Canada, Japan, New Zealand, Russia, Singapore and the United States are next on its list for global expansion, and could later launch in Argentina, Chile, Colombia, Hong Kong, India, Indonesia, Korea, Malaysia, Mexico,

Philippines, Saudi Arabia, South Africa, Taiwan, Thailand, Ukraine and Vietnam thanks to its Visa partnership.

'The new global agreement with Visa is timely for Revolut as we move into a number of new markets to offer even more consumers the control, flexibility and innovative features that our European customers have been benefiting from for years,' said Nikolay Storonsky, CEO and Founder of Revolut. The news came along with Storonsky revealing a huge hiring surge over the next 12 months. 'We are around 1,500 people now and by summer next year we plan to be around 5,000,' Storonsky told Reuters.

Questions

For one of the specified new markets that Revolut plans to enter, conduct an external analysis to identify and evaluate the most critical factors likely to impact on its operations in the chosen country.

Recommend and justify the most appropriate foreign market entry strategy that Revolut should adopt to enter the chosen country.

Critically assess whether the company should adopt a standardization, adaptation or hybrid strategy in the marketing of its products in the chosen country.

Bibliography

Aaker, D.A. (2004). *Building Strong Brands*. Sydney: Simon & Shuster

American Alliances for Audiences and Artists. Available at: www.4aarts.org. Accessed 22 August 2020

American Marketing Association (n.d). 'Dictionary', available at: wwwama.org/resources/Pages/Dictionary-aspx. Accessed 12 January 2020

Ansoff, I (1957). 'Strategies for Diversification'. *Harvard Business Review*, 35 (5), 113–24

Armstrong, G. and Kotler, P (2018).*Marketing: An Introduction*. London: Pearson

Barney, J. (2002). *Gaining and Sustaining Competitive Advantage*. 2nd Ed. Upper Saddle River, NJ: Prentice Hall

Belen del Rio, A., Vasquez, R. and Iglesia, V. (2001). 'The effects of brand associations on customer response'. *Journal of Consumer Marketing*, 18 (5): 410–25

Bennett, P.D. (1988), *Dictionary of Marketing Terms*. The American Marketing Association, Chicago, IL, p. 18

Berry, L. (1980). 'Services Marketing is Different'. *Business*, 30 (3): 52–6

Bovee, .C.L (1992). *Contemporary Advertising*. New York: Abe Books

BusinessofApps (2020). Revolut Statistics and Usage Data. Available at: https://www.businessofapps.com/data/revolut-statistics/. Accessed December 2020

BusinessofApps (2020). Tiktok Revenue and Usage Statistics. Available at: https://www.businessofapps.com/data/tik-tok-statistics/. Accessed December 2020

Chaffey, D. and Smith, P. (2012). *Remix in Emarketing Excellence: Planning and Optimising Your Digital Marketing (Emarketing Essentials)* (4th Edn). Oxford: Routledge

Chartered Institute of Marketing (n.d). Marketing Glossary. Available at: www.cim.co.uk (accessed 12 January 2020)

Chartered Institute of Public Relations (2013). 'What is PR?' Available at: www.cipr.co.uk.content/careers-cpd/careers-pr/what-pr (accessed 13 April 2020)

Chung, H.F., Wang, C.L. & Huang, P.H. (2012) 'A contingency approach to International Marketing strategy and decision-making structure among just exporting firms'. *International Marketing Review*, Vol.29, Issue 1, 2012

Dibb, S. and Simkin, L. (2008). *Marketing Briefs*. London: Elsevier Butterworth Heinemann

Digiday (2020). 'A regular drum beat of content: How brands like Chobani are using TikTok to reach new audiences'. Available at: https://digiday.com/marketing/using-tiktok-to-reach-new-audiences/. Accessed December 2020

Doyle, P. (2017). *Marketing Management and Strategy*. Harlow: Prentice Hall

Eco-Refill Systems Corporation: Available at: ecorefillsystems.com (Accessed 13 May 2020)

Egan, J. (2007). *Marketing Communications*. Hampshire: Cengage

Ehrenberg, A. (1974), 'Repetitive Advertising and the Consumer', *Journal of Advertising Research*, 14, 25–34.

Ehrenberg, A.S.C. & Scriven, J. (1997) 'Added values or propensities to buy?' *Admap*, September.

Ehrenberg, A.S.C., Barnard, J.R. & Scriven, J. (1997) 'Differentiation or salience?' *Journal of Advertising Research*, Nov-Dec

Engel, J., Blackwell, R., and Miniard, P. (2006). *Consumer Behaviour*, 9th Edition. Fort Worth, TX: Dryden Press

Evinex (2020). *Mobile Marketing: The Definitive Guide in 2020*. Available at: www.evinex.com/ mobile-marketing. Accessed 20 September 2020

Gronroos, C. (1997). 'From marketing mix to relationship marketing: towards a paradigm shift in marketing'. *Management Decision*, 35 (4): 322–9

Grove, S.J., Fisk, R.P. and Joby, J. (2003). 'The future of services marketing: forecasts from ten service experts'. *Journal of Services Marketing*. 17 (2): 107–21

Grunig, J. and Hunt, T. (1984). *Managing Public Relations*. London: Thomson Learning

Gummerson, E. (2008b). *Total Relationship Marketing* (3rd Edn). Oxford: Butterworth Heinemann

Hootsuite (2020). 25 Twitter Stats All Marketers Need to Know in 2020. Available at: https://blog.hootsuite.com/twitter-statistics/. Accessed December 2020

Jones, J.P. (1990). 'Advertising: strong or weak force? Two views oceans apart'. *Journal of Advertising*, 9 (3): 233-46

Kaplan, R.S and Norton, D.P. (1992). 'The Balanced Scorecard: Measures that Drive Performance'. *Harvard Business Review*, Jan–Feb, 71–79

Keller, K.L and Swaminathan, V. (2020). *Strategic Brand Management*. Fifth Edition. Pearson: Global Edition. United Kingdom

Kohli, G. and Sharma, R.D. (2009). 'Market Orientation: the construct, research propositions and managerial implications'. *Journal of Marketing*, 54 (April), 1–18

Kotler, P. (2003). *Marketing Insights from A–Z: 80 Concepts Every Marketer Needs to Know*. New York: John Wiley & Sons

Levitt, T (1960). 'Marketing Myopia'. *Harvard Business Review* Jul/Aug 28, 45–56

Levitt, T. (1965). 'Exploit the Product Life Cycle'. *Harvard Business Review* 43 Nov/ Dec: 80 (4): 81–94

Marketing Charts (2020). 'Consumers Turned More to These Online Services During the Pandemic'. Available at: https://www.marketingcharts.com/. Accessed December 2020

Masterson, R., Phillips, N. and Pickton, D. (2017). *Marketing: An Introduction*. Los Angeles: Sage

McDonald, M. and Wilson, H. (2011). *Marketing Plans: How to Prepare Them, How to Use Them* (7th Edition). Chichester: John Wiley

Moorman, C. and Day, G.S. (2016). 'Organizing for Marketing Excellence'. *Journal of Marketing*, 80 (6): 6–35

Omnicore Agency (2020). Twitter by the Numbers: Stats, Demographics & Fun Facts. Available at: https://www.omnicoreagency.com/twitter-statistics/. Accessed December 2020

Paliwoda, S.J. and Thomas, N.J. (1990). *International Marketing* (3rd Edition). Oxford: Butterworth Heinemann

Parasuraman, A., Zeithaml, V. and Berry, L. (1985): 'A Conceptual Model for Service Quality and Its Implications for Future Research'. *Journal of Retailing*, fall, 41–50

Peters, T.J and Waterman, R.H. (2004). *In Search of Excellence*, Second Edition. London: Pacific Books

Place Me Corporation. Available at: www.placemeliving.com. Accessed 12 July 2020

Porter, M. (1980). 'Industry Structure and Competitive Strategy: Keys to Profitability'. *Financial Analysts*, 36 (4), 30–41

Porter, M.E (1985). *Competitive Advantage: Creating and Sustaining Superior Performance*. Glencoe, IL: Free Press

Poulis, K. & Poulis, E. (2013) 'The influence of intra-national cultural heterogeneity on product standardization and adaptation: A qualitative study'. *International Marketing Review*, Vol.6, Issue 3, 2013

Ryan, D., and Jones, C. (2018). *Understanding Digital Marketing*. London: Kogan Page

Solomon, M.R., Bamossy, G., Askegaard, S. and Hogg, M.K. (2010). *Consumer Behaviour: A European Perspective* (4th Edition) Harlow: Pearson Education

Sproutsocial (2020). Facebook statistics every marketer should know in 2020. Available at: https://sproutsocial.com/insights/facebook-stats-for-marketers/. Accessed December 2020.

TikTok: Statistics and Background (2020); Available on: https://blog.hubspot.com/marketing/tiktok-stats. Accessed October 2020

Tuten, T.L. and Solomon, M.R. (2015). *Social Media Marketing* (2nd Edition). London: Sage

Vallaster, C. and von Wallpach, S. (2013). 'An online discursive inquiry into the social dynamics of multi-stakeholder brand meaning co-creation'. *Journal of Business Research*, 66 (9): 1505–15

Woodcock, N, Starkey, M. and Stone, M. (2000). *The Customer Management Scorecard: A Strategic Framework for Benchmarking Performance against Best Practice*. London: Business Intelligence

Index